The Healing Power of
MUDRAS
THE YOGA OF THE HANDS

Rajendar Menen

SINGING
DRAGON

SINGING DRAGON
LONDON AND PHILADELPHIA

First published by Singing Dragon in 2010
an imprint of Jessica Kingsley Publishers
116 Pentonville Road
London N1 9JB, UK
and
400 Market Street, Suite 400
Philadelphia, PA 19106, USA

www.singing-dragon.com

Copyright © Original English Edition: M/s. Pustak Mahal, India.
First published in India by Pustak Mahal in 2004
Published in Great Britain by Singing Dragon in 2010

Library of Congress Cataloging in Publication Data
A CIP catalog record for this book is available from the Library of Congress

British Library Cataloguing in Publication Data
A CIP catalogue record for this book is available from the British Library

ISBN 978 1 84819 043 6

Printed and bound in the United States by
Thomson-Shore, 7300 Joy Road, Dexter, MI 48130

Dedication

This book is dedicated to Prabhadevi, Suzanne, Pondicherry, G-304 Sameer and Hard Disc. There are several fellow travellers, and the wind, the rain and the sun, and His grace that made their presence felt every moment of my life as I continued to enter this vast, uncharted space of natural healing. May the grace encompass us all.

Most important, this book is dedicated to my mother, who nursed me through crises, weathered my innumerable idiosyncrasies with stoic calm and gave me the genes to fight for a better world.

Acknowledgements

This book would not have been possible without the help of several practitioners of Mudra healing. Not much documentation is available but I tapped all sources I could lay my hands on. A very special note of gratitude to Gertrude Hirschi for her humbling and illuminating insights into the subject. She is blessed and is a true Messiah of healing. It is unfortunate that all these truisms from ancient India need the western world to document, perfect and improve upon. But now that they have done it, let the seeds scatter and pollinate the land. This is sharing at its profoundest.

Contents

Preface

Life is a series of endless miracles which keep happening in our lives almost all the time. They happen so effortlessly and without warning that they often pass by unrecognised. They visit the humblest as well as the most powerful, without prejudice or favour, and defy all logic and rational explanation.

This is my fourth book on healing. In a career spanning over two decades as a journalist and writer, and having led a peripatetic life spanning continents, I have been privy to the most mundane, the colossally bizarre, the malignantly morbid, the ludicrously humorous and the profoundly soul elevating. I have spent quality time on the streets and in brothels and the corridors of the dispossessed while attempting to document their angst and joy. Miracles kept happening in their lives and in mine, in fact all around us, but we simply bypassed their pedigree, remained connected to the real world of cause and effect, and pronounced our everyday judgements.

But it was while researching the process of healing that I fully realised the miracles that were happening in our lives almost all the time. Our bodies are a miracle, birth and death are miracles, and the whole process of healing is a miracle. It is easy to pass it all off as 'holistic healing', the 'mind-body connection' and with other similar jargon. Conventional and alternative medicine men also take recourse in rational explanations, but they know that, beyond a point, remissions happen and healing occurs without easy explanation. It is then passed off as divine intervention.

Over the years I have also experimented with several healing techniques. Most of them work, but for different people and at different times. If they don't work for a particular person, it doesn't mean that the technique or the therapy is wrong. It is just that the person and the time are not right... or that the person is not yet ready to be the medium.

I have also been practising yoga and meditation for over a decade and have been privileged to spend huge quality time with several masters. There are several days during the practice when your entire being is elevated and you feel an endless joy floating through you. If you were to jot down the period with pen and paper, the milestones would be no different from the saddest periods of your life or even the most ordinary ones. Yet, there is an inexplicable joy that transports your being into a cascade of sheer ecstasy.

Mudras – as you will read in the book – are simple, free and easy to do. They can be done anywhere and they heal the body. I am not, at any stage, suggesting that you do away with your doctor and his prescriptions. But regular practise of Mudras has been shown to heal conclusively.

Several explanations are offered for the healing that takes place. But as you get regular with the practice, you begin to knock at the doors of an inner spirituality. With time, you are transformed from deep within at the cellular level. You begin to respect your body more and look at all life with new admiration. Slowly, you begin to give in to the powerful and comforting embrace of existence. You know, somehow, that it will take care of you.

Welcome to Mudras, healing, and the new you!

—*Rajendar Menen*

Understanding Mudras

It is widely believed that the human structure is a miniature form of the universe that is made up of five elements – fire, air, water, earth and sky. These elements are present in fixed proportions and even the slightest imbalance of any of these can be disastrous.

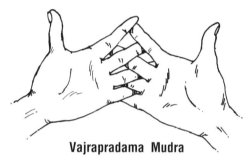

Vajrapradama Mudra

Mudras help normalise the five elements in the human body. Nature has made the human body self-sufficient, self-contained and almost perfect. But a human being is prone to innumerable pressures. The food we eat, the air we breathe, the water we drink, and even our thoughts are in no way compatible with what can be called the ideal way of life. Since there is no equilibrium, as the body and mind are at war with so many external and internal pressures, we fall ill. Our bodies are in a constant state of flux, recharging and rebalancing all the time. When there is an imbalance we fall ill.

The balance we aspire to and need is a tricky business. Anything can upset it. From loneliness, break-ups in relationships, shifting house, even examination failure and not reaching peer group expectations, to name just a few, to the insidious attacks from viruses and germs that room with us on this planet. All mandatory props for a healthy life have been devalued today. The water we drink, the food we eat, and even the air we breathe has been compromised. We have moved far away from nature, and the germs and the human body that host them have also mutated several times. It is so very easy now to lose balance, to fall from grace so to say.

We will now examine how Mudras influence the human being. The five fingers of the hand represent the elements. The thumb represents fire, the forefinger air, the middle finger sky, the third or ring finger earth and the fourth finger water.

"Hands have a power of their own," says Acharya Keshav Dev, a well-known practitioner. "Through the regular practise of various Mudras, a person can control his life."

Director of the Vivekanand Yogashram in Delhi, soft spoken, articulate and extremely knowledgeable, the Acharya can talk endlessly and with authority on the science of Mudras. About *hasta mudras* (hand postures), the Acharya says that there is a tremendous flow of energy in our hands and each finger represents one of the five elements – the thumb is *agni* (fire), the forefinger is *vayu* (air), the middle finger is *akash* (ether), the ring finger is *prithvi* (earth) and the little finger is *jal* (water). "The roots of all diseases lie in an imbalance of one of the five elements and can be corrected with medicines, willpower and Mudras," he says. "The science of Mudras is one of the finest gifts of yoga to the cause of human welfare."

The Acharya explains that Mudras are universal and suitable for everyone. They can be practised for half-an-hour everyday. It is advisable to sit cross-legged while doing a Mudra, but he adds that the Mudra will not be rendered ineffective even if it is done while on a stroll with the hands casually tucked in the pockets, fingers folded in a particular Mudra. They can also be done lying down, and so are easy to do.

10

Mudras never generate an excess of energy, he continues. Like a thermostat, they simply seek an optimal balancing of *prana*. So the next time you are ailing, remember it may just be an instance of maladjusted *prana* and an innocuous sleight of hand could be the cure!

Mudras are yoga movements involving only the arms and hands. They are extremely easy to do, but so powerful that they can transform one's life. They liberate the energy locked within your body – in energy channels called *nadis* and energy centres called *chakras*. Mudras help create inner peace and inner strength, eliminate fatigue and anxiety, protect physical and emotional health, help transcend stress, depression, guilt and anger, calm the mind and sharpen intuition, and promote happiness, love, prosperity and longevity.

Considering the ease with which Mudras can be done, the little time and space they consume, and the enormous benefits associated with them at no extra cost whatsoever, it may just be the valuable tool to good health and mental peace that we need so urgently in a life that is so frenetically hurtling away from any type of balance. No previous experience with yoga is needed to do Mudras. You don't have to be an athlete or be youthful either. In fact, Mudras can be done even from the sick bed. All you need to do is move your arms and hands freely and pay attention to your breathing. This is as simple as it can get. And you enrich your life – wherever you are – in as little as a few minutes a day.

In a modest, nondescript apartment at Juhu Gully in suburban Mumbai, 64-year-old Ramesh Shah practises Mudras everyday and also teaches them to those who are interested. "It is a simple way of preserving one's health and my goal is to spread the message to all those who need it," he says.

Ramesh Shah

11

Shah, who used to run "a mechanical workshop", suffered from high blood pressure and gastric complaints. He met a Mudra teacher who explained the Mudras to him. Shah tried it, was cured of his problems, and there was no looking back. "It is a free medicine," he says happily. "You don't have to go to hospital. You save a lot of money."

Serene and scholarly, Shah explains *Pran Mudra* or the Mudra for life energy: "Bend the little and ring fingers so that their tips touch the tip of the thumb. As simple as that." The benefits include an increase in the life force, improvement in eyesight, blood circulation and immune function. "In the *Varuna Mudra*, put the tips of the thumb and little finger together," he says. "It will cure impurities of the blood and skin and stomach problems."

The *Gyan Mudra* is equally simple and effective. "Gently touch the thumb with the index finger. This will help in improving the power of the mind. In the *Jalodhar Naashak Mudra* the little finger should touch the mount of the thumb and the thumb should touch the little finger. This Mudra is good for water retention in the body," Shah avers.

Ramesh Shah claims to know over 45 Mudras. He believes that no particular pose is essential for Mudras but it is "good to place a mat or cloth on the floor and sit in *Padmasan* or *Vajrasan* positions. But Mudras can be done standing, sitting and even walking".

He then talks about the *Akash Mudra*: "Touch the middle finger with the thumb. It increases the person's intuition, cures calcium deficiency, tooth and ear problems."

(We detail all the Mudras comprehensively later on in the book. Please remember that though Mudras are effective and useful in treating various health problems, don't stop medication without consulting your physician. Practitioners often mention patients who started the Mudras and then slowly discontinued the medication without any adverse effects. In

fact, they say that over a period of time the Mudras cure the patients completely. But please check with your attending doctor before discontinuing any medication.)

After almost a decade of practise, Ramesh Shah believes that *Gyan Mudra*, *Vayu Mudra* and *Pran Mudra* can be done everyday. "The other Mudras should be done only when you are suffering from a certain problem. They should be done for a maximum of fifteen minutes three times a day," he advises.

Shah believes that it is best to do the Mudras on an empty stomach but "*Vayu Mudra* can be done soon after eating as it eliminates gastric problems".

Shah concludes with *Vayu Mudra*: "It is incredible. The body is controlled by five elements. All the energy is in the fingers. Through different combinations of the fingers, we can not only control these elements but also cure many diseases."

Ancient Healing Rediscovered

Not far away, in Malad, another Mumbai suburb, is 62-year-old Yogi Kumar who teaches yoga and healing Mudras. He was in the garments business and took to teaching yoga full-time after retirement a few years ago.

"I have over 40 years' experience," he reveals. "I learnt yoga at Mathura. In fact, I started meditation from the age of four. My father was also a yoga teacher. I am blessed with intuition. Even at a young age I could guess all the questions in my examination papers. I knew I had some power and I kept working hard at it to reach a position of strength. After my professional life was stabilised I thought I should spread the message of good health in society."

A vegetarian, Yogi Kumar does yoga and over 20 Mudras every day. "It takes over an hour-and-a-half," he says. "I then travel all over the city to meet patients. I charge about three hundred rupees per patient per day but it all depends on the distance I have to travel and the type of disease I am treating."

Yogi Kumar insists that any disease can be cured through Mudras. He says that he has treated asthma, arthritis, cardiac problems, kidney disease, sexual problems, migraines, back complaints and even the dreaded and largely incurable blood cancer.

"This is not a boast," he insists. "There are two types of

Mudras – body Mudras and hand postures. Mudras are ancient. It began with Lord Shiva and it is all documented in his conversations with his consort Parvati. It is an ancient science and is easy and free. No medicines are needed and the cure is hundred per cent. But the patient should follow my instructions to the letter. I am very strict about that. If all my instructions are obeyed, I can guarantee a cure."

There are other practitioners too spread out in different parts of India. But the knowledge of Mudras is scanty and there is no common thread that runs through them. Since healing through Mudras is unconventional medicine at best and receives no official patronage, it is left to isolated believers to propagate it. Like several other healing systems that originated in the folds of time, Mudras have not been subject to scientific scrutiny. There is no documentation either but verbal testimonies to its efficacy are rampant and that's why the usefulness of Mudras is still alive and in our midst.

This is a common problem with all the ancient healing techniques which are not profit centres. An old and rich civilisation like India has several such healing techniques but they are constantly 'discovered' by the western world, patented abroad by them and resold to us!

As I write this, reports have streamed in that *Jeevani* – the energy herb from Kerala that was discovered by local tribals – has now been patented by the west. This has happened to several other ayurvedic formulations as well. Even Indian dance and music has been researched extensively and given new dimensions. Ditto with yoga, massage techniques and other holistic remedies. Mudras have already entered the western world. It won't be long before the whole world gets to know of them in their new, revised and more potent forms.

"It is only because there is no money in it that it is not well known or developed," claim practitioners. "There is big money in allopathy and hospitals. Who will promote something which is free?"

The flip side is that without documentation and further research, the science may hit a roadblock in terms of evolution. Mudras heal. There is no question about that. But delving into its methodology and formulating newer techniques to harness the gigantic power in our fingers may certainly be invaluable.

All the ancient healing techniques like ayurveda, massage, yoga and the like have been subject to intensive research. The human body has also changed over time. We hope that after reading this book, efforts are made to propagate and document a healing methodology which is ideal for a developing country – it is free, takes hardly any time, can be done anywhere, requires no gadgetry, cures almost all diseases, and helps keep the body and mind in a continuous state of calm. It originated in India and has lived with us for thousands of years. Can there be better reasons to popularise Mudras and make them a household healing regimen?

Some Interesting Facts

All godly and superhuman persons like Lord Mahavir, Gautam Buddha, Adi Shankaracharya and others would remain in these Mudras. Mudras are simple yogic functions with enormous significance. Detailed descriptions of Mudras are found in *Tantra Shastra*, *Upasana Shastra, Nritya Shastra*, and several other ancient treatises.

❑ Mudras can bring about miraculous changes and improvement in our body.

❑ Mudras generate power to provide peace and happiness.

❑ Mudras are miraculous remedies. They provide instant relief in many illnesses.

❑ Mudras can cure almost any ailment from simple earache to heart attack.

❑ Mudras help in moulding the physical, mental and even the moral aspects of an individual.

❑ Some Mudras can balance the elements of the body within 45 minutes while others act within a few seconds.

❑ Practise of some Mudras on a regular basis can cure insomnia, arthritis and memory loss.

❑ Mudras bring about a fundamental revision of the destructive changes in the human body. They also develop piety and a courteous disposition.

❑ Mudras help in Kundalini Yoga to awaken the cosmic energy.

✧★✧

Mudras and Dance

Mudras or 'sign language' is the most important element of dance. So much is conveyed in dance and, yet, no copious sentences are uttered. If dance is the language, Mudras are the words used in that language. Mudras are formed with the fingers of either a single hand or both the hands. The dancer conveys whatever he or she wants to and effectively too with various contortions of the arms and the fingers. All dance is evocative and rich in articulation and yet nothing much is said verbally. All communication is with signs, gestures and movements. It is powerful body language that is universal and floral in expression.

There are two kinds of Mudras. One is formed by the use of a single hand and the other is formed by using both the hands. *Asamyukta hastam* means single-hand Mudras and *Samyukta hastam* refers to Mudras formed by using both the hands. *Samyukta* literally means 'joined'. There are 28 single-hand Mudras and 24 double-hand ones. Let's look at a few single-hand Mudras.

Bend the right ring finger to half its length. Let it touch the thumb. Keep the other three fingers vertically erect. This is the *Mayura Mudra* or the peacock sign. It represents the peacock and also expresses vomiting, pushing back one's hair, applying 'tilak' on one's forehead, taking water from a holy river and sprinkling on one's head, teaching (*upadesa*), and several other messages too, which also includes the most common one of appreciation. As you can see, a simple gesture, an almost insignificant movement of the finger, can say so much.

Let's take it further. The opposite feelings of friendship and enmity are also expressed with a single double-hand Mudra. The only difference is in the fingers. Close all the fingers of both hands, except the forefingers. Bend both the forefingers like hooks and place them opposite each other. Move them away, in opposite directions and they are like two enemies facing each other. Now fold all the fingers except the little fingers of both hands. Bend them to form a hook and place them against each other. Now you represent two friends. In both these Mudras, the left hand is held above the right hand.

Without the use of words, these Mudras convey so much. Imagine what a combination of them would say!

A powerful example of the use of Mudras is in *Kathakali* ("story play"), the globally acclaimed classical dance drama of Kerala, which dates to the 17th century and is deeply rooted in Hindu mythology. *Kathakali* has a unique combination of literature, music, painting, acting and dance.

Kathakali draws heavily from drama and is danced with elaborate masks and costumes. It is both emotive and narrative and combines dance with dialogue to bring myth and legend to life in the temple courtyards of Kerala. The dancers use their stunning costumes and make-up, to the accompaniment of drums and vocalists, to create various moods and emotions.

Kathakali is spellbinding. It has a harmonious combination of literature (*Sahithyam*), music (*Sangeetham*), painting (*Chithram*), acting (*Natyam*) and dance (*Nritham*). The costumes are vivid and colourful, the facial make-up is done by the artist himself and a distinct headgear made of wood is worn during the play. The *Aharya* (make-up) has many faces like *Pacha, Kathi, Thadi, and Minukku* etc.

In *Kathakali* the dancers do not speak, but their hand movements or Mudras, along with facial expressions, speak several volumes. Frenzied drumming and a preamble-like musical note called *Thiranottam* pitches this exquisite form of dance, which lasts all through the night, into the realm of fantasy.

There are 24 basic Mudras (hand gestures) in the *Hasthalakshana Deepika*, the Book of Hand Gestures, which *Kathakali* follows. There are *Asamyukta Mudras* (with one hand) and *Samyukta Mudras* (with both hands) in each basic Mudra. The Mudras and their separations total 470 symbols.

Kathakali is only one example. But all other dance forms too are replete with the silent eloquence of Mudras.

Padma Shree Dr Kanak Rele, who runs the Nalanda Dance Research Centre at Juhu in Mumbai, explains that it is not possible to count the number of *hastas* or Mudras in dance. "Each dance style has its own system and categories of *hastas*," she says. "But each system has basic *hastas* from which a number of different *hastas* are created by permutations and combinations. For example, every dance style uses the basic *hasta* called *Pataaka* (flag). They may be performed in different ways by using the fingers vis-à-vis the palm in different ways. In *Kathakali*, which uses the Sanskrit text, *Hastalakshanadeepika*, *Pataaka* is to be

Dr Kanak Rele

held by keeping the palm straight, the fingers completely extended and then bending the ring finger at the middle joint. It can be held by both the hands, which would be called *Samyukta*. If it is done with only one hand it would then be called *Asamyukta*."

Winner of several awards, Dr Rele is well known for re-establishing the exquisitely lyrical dance of *Mohini Attam* and for introducing new vistas to research in classical dance. She is also credited with pioneering work into the dynamics of Indian dance, which resulted in her theory on the Body Kinetics of dance.

"The usages of *Samyukta* are many," she continues. "By placing each hand at different places in the spaces around the body one can create the sun, king, elephant, lion, *torana* (flower garlands for doors), bullock, crocodile and so on. With the *Asamyukta*, the language of dance continues. It is different. *Bharata Natyam* uses the Sanskrit text *Abhinayadarpana* in which the *Pataaka hasta* is to be held by keeping the palm straight with all the fingers extended and the thumb touching the palm. So with permutations and combinations, hundreds of *hastas* or Mudras are created."

The origins of Mudras are not really clear. Most dance teachers and Mudra practitioners agree that it is ancient but there is no consensus on dates. "*Hastas* originated when the need for stylisation in a dramatic presentation was felt," says Dr Kanak Rele. "This stylisation was codified so that a single system originally arose to encompass the different parts of ancient India. This made the practice universal. Since there are no words spoken in dance, the dancer has to interpret the words of the song with *hastas* and suitable facial expressions."

Hastas are very eloquent and are profound in their communication. They are the words of dance. They form alphabets, and their permutations, as has been illustrated, create words for nouns, actions, qualities and things. "They can mirror life or even articulate abstractions," points out Dr Rele. "These *hastas* are individual words which are to be used appropriately in sentences. So each sentence will have different *hastas* strung together."

Mudras are very Indian. They probably spread to other parts of the world from here. "In south-east Asian dances one finds a few rudimentary or truncated *hastas*. I have seen some symbolic, standardised hand movements in Hawaiian dances, which are not really *hastas*. But they are not found anywhere else in the world," says Dr Kanak Rele with some finality. After immersing herself in dance for over four decades with aplomb, she should know.

Meaning and Purpose of Mudras

The word *Mudra* literally means *seal*. It has a number of different connotations in yoga, which include *bandhas* (locks) and meditation practices. However, Mudras are most commonly associated with hand gestures. The fingers are related to different types of energies, and when they are brought together in specific ways, they produce subtle effects.

Mudras can help balance the flow of energy through the *nadis* that nourish our internal organs. They can also be performed to achieve specific states of consciousness. They also help eliminate negative thought forms and aid mood elevation.

Now that the basic introduction is done, we present a few Mudras developed by Kareena who teaches yoga and leads energy and posture workshops in the United States. Normally, no specific positions are required but in this case they should ideally be practised with the spine and head erect. The eyes are focused downward toward the nostrils or at the Sun centre between the eyebrows to activate the third eye. It may also be helpful if the feet touch the floor or if the practitioner assumes a half or full lotus position. These Mudras are easy to do and can change our lives forever if done regularly.

Mudra for Trust

Lift hands overhead and place right palm over back of left hand. (Reverse hands for men.) Elbows bend softly and shoulders press down away from ears. Imagine creating a triangle over your *crown chakra* in an attempt to connect to it. Breathe short, fast breaths of fire, while focusing on the navel, to build inner trust.

Mudra for Joy

Bend elbows and open arms to side. Position hands at shoulder level with palms facing forward. Press the little and ring fingers down into palms and cross your thumb tightly over them. Lift middle and index fingers straight up toward the heavens like the peace sign. Inhale slowly for eight counts. Exhale for eight counts. Smile as you feel the glow of your inner light.

Mudra for Recharging

Fist your right hand with thumb pointing upwards. Wrap your left palm around the right hand's fist, thumb pointing upwards. Touch the two thumbs together, straighten elbows and push arms and hands away from chest. Feel the left hand resisting the strong push of the right fist. Push shoulders back to increase resistance. Avoid hunching shoulders; keep chest and rib cage lifted. Focusing eyes on thumbs, inhale slowly for eight counts and exhale for eight counts. Feel energy radiating from base of spine into hands and arms as you recharge.

The Practise of Visualisation

The power of visualisation is well known. Powerful positive visualisation done everyday can empower the practitioner to perform extraordinary feats. One's personal window to the world emanates from self-esteem and self-belief. If you feel you can, YOU CAN. Visualisation is not only about Mudras. They go a long way even in everyday life.

The *chakras* are regarded as the centres of psychic energy. If you visualise with clarity and intensity, you can become what you visualise. Of course, it is not as simple as that. Miracles would take place if visualisation were so easy. But with a great deal of sustained and honest practise, a person can become well and whole by simply visualising wellness.

Similarly, if you visualise sickness, you promote an aura of sickness within you and literally fall ill. All of us live a portion of our lives in fantasy. We, at times, start believing what we are intrinsically not, almost to the point of delusion, but with sustained affirmation, we even become it. So much for the power of the mind. It creates matter, and then decomposes it with the power of thought.

Let's move on to more spiritual aspects relevant to yoga and the Mudras. For example, when you contemplate and visualise the earth centre your whole being becomes that earth centre. When you become one with space, the body is said to "disintegrate". In infinite space, one sees

25

what can only be described as "lightning", or the *ajna chakra*. With well-directed visualisation even chronic problems can be cured both of the mind and the body because the connection between the two is profound.

You simply have to merge completely with whatever it is that you are visualising and strongly affirm positivity at a deep cellular level. A feeling of bliss will consume you. You will radiate joy, and be one with your inner and outer selves. With the right mind-body connection, holistic healing will be born.

Recent research has shown that people with depression have increased mortality after heart attacks and it is not linked to smoking or sedentary behaviour. The part of the nervous system that regulates heart rates works differently in depressed people, and their abnormal platelets may cause arterial blockage.

For centuries, the mind-body connection has come in for intense scrutiny. First, the pineal gland was considered the link between body and soul, and later it was the pituitary gland. In the new medical model, the mind and body are seen as parts of a single system. We now believe that nature has used the same molecules for a multitude of purposes in both brain and body. When something goes awry with their production in the brain, it will show in other body parts as well.

Today, new technology can visualise the functioning of the depressed brain. Areas that are barely working appear as ragged holes. Body functions collapse under depression and stress. The immune system breaks down and we fall prey to innumerable diseases. Take a break, get happy ad the body gets revitalised. So often, people fall sick and yet their medical tests show that nothing is wrong with them. The medical fraternity is at a loss to explain this. Then, with time, the emotions get sorted out, and they are inexplicably well again.

Animals express this body-mind connection without inhibition.

Gertrude Hirschi, an authority on Mudras, writes about the visualisation necessary for the *Lotus Mudra*. She says, "Imagine the bud of a lotus flower in your heart. Every time you inhale, the flower opens a bit more – until it finally is completely open and can absorb the full sunlight into itself. It lets itself be filled with light, lightness, warmth, love, desire and joy." Along with this is the affirmation: "I open myself to nature; I open myself to the good that exists in every human being; and I open myself to the Divine so that I will be richly blessed."

To charge oneself with energy, Gertrude recommends the following visualisation while doing the *Shiva linga*. "Imagine that your left hand is a mortar and your right hand is a pestle. During the first breaths, mentally let whatever makes you sick fall like dark pebbles into your left hand. With the edge of your right hand, grind everything into the finest dust, which you then blow away from your hand like fine sand. Afterwards, remain seated for a while and let healing energy flow into the bowl formed by your hand (your energy reservoir) through the right thumb." Fervently speak the following affirmation several times: "Healing light illuminate every cell of my body, dissolve everything that should be dissolved, and build up what must be built up again. Thank you!"

While doing the *Joint Mudra* for more flexibility, Gertrude says, "Visualise images where you completely enjoy your flexibility; you easily and freely move your legs and arms, feet and hands, head and neck. You see yourself as a dancer, athlete or performer and feel how your energy flows and your mood improves." The affirmation she suggests: "I enjoy my flexibility. It uplifts my soul and stimulates my mind."

In this manner, every Mudra is accompanied by profound visualisation and an affirmation. All the visualisations and affirmations are Mudra-specific. But they are all positive, uplifting and energising and take you to newer reaches of self-discovery and growth. It's about telling yourself to believe in what you thought was impossible all this while. It is similar to whatever else you do in life. Faith works wonders. Adopt a winner's attitude. Believe that you will come out on top, and you will. Focus on your weaknesses and failure, and you are beaten. So why not do suitable healing Mudras, visualise wellness, affirm it, and come out whole and well and the better for it?

Visualisation is used in several other spheres as well. It is an important tool while recuperating from surgery. It's an intrinsic asset for achievers in any field and most particularly in sport where one coasts along during the 'wall' phase and lifts oneself in the 'zone' to superhuman effort. The loneliness of the marathon runner is legendary, a loneliness wherein he lives only with the dream. It is common with all sport; the more dangerous it gets, the greater the role of the mind. Even in war, battle indoctrination transforms a simple goatherd into a fighting machine. So much for the mind!!

There are some techniques laid out in the *Hatha Yoga Pradipika* and the *Gerandha Samhita*, which aid visualisation in *chakra* meditation.

Practising Mudras

Many Mudras are normally associated only with the hands. Several Mudras have been preserved in Indian dancing or as symbols, the most famous of which is the *Chit-mudra*, which denotes *chit* or wisdom of the highest consciousness. But for the yogi the word *Mudra* translates as *seal*; the 'seal' that closes and safeguards.

Mudras are said to awaken the *kundalini* energy. They can be practised either before or after other yoga practices like *pranayama* or *asanas*. Mudras can be practised without any difficulty. The practice of *maha-mudra* is especially easy to do. *Maha-mudra* is performed to aid visualisation of the *sushumna*.

To perform it, simply sit on the ground, and place the left heel on the perineum, being careful not to sit on it. The right leg is kept straight and at a right angle to the body. Clasp your right foot with both hands, not merely touching the foot but holding it firmly. Concentrate within, turning your attention to the eyebrow centre.

Now fix your gaze inwards, and clearly visualise the *sushumna nadi* as a radiant shell running vertically through the centre of your body from top to bottom. Inhale. Do *jalandhara-bandha* (dropping the chin and pressing it firmly to the chest), and hold the breath, continuing to visualise the *sushumna nadi*. The visualisation is only of the psychic tube and not of the individual *chakras*. Since the heel of the foot is on the perineum, and since your attention has also been focused on the eyebrow centre, you are immediately aware of where the *sushumna* begins and ends.

After holding the breath to your capacity, raise the chin and exhale slowly. This is the first half of the procedure. Repeat it but this time place the left leg out straight and the right foot on the perineum. This is the second half of one complete round of the *maha-mudra*. If necessary, do several complete rounds of *maha-mudra*. It may be necessary to visualise the *sushumna* clearly.

After finishing with *maha-mudra*, perform what is called *maha-bandha*. Place the left heel against the perineum. Place the right foot on the left thigh. Inhale, do the chin lock, and place the palms on the floor. As part of the *maha-bandha*, you should perform the *mula-bandha*, contracting the muscles to close or "bind" the anus while also contracting the muscles in such a way so as to pull up the alimentary canal. This *mula-bandha* must be firmly kept while you continue with the *maha-bandha*. Contemplation is of the eyebrow centre. And as in *maha-mudra*, you visualise the *sushumna*. As before, you raise the chin, and exhale slowly.

Finally, still assuming the *maha-bandha*, you perform the *maha-vedha*. Take a deep breath and hold it and, while dropping the chin again into *jalandhara-bandha*, you lift and raise your buttocks off the ground, your two palms pushing you from the ground. Then drop the buttocks, letting it gently strike the floor. *Maha-mudra*, *maha-bandha*, and *maha-vedha* are all three parts of one exercise and are practised together.

All three produce some effects upon the perineum. These are performed because they help create sensitivity about the beginning of the *sushumna*. The eyebrow centre is the terminus of the *sushumna*. The concentration should be free to move through the entire field of the *sushumna* because the *sushumna* is not just top, middle, and bottom, but one field, one *sushumna*! Therefore, this meditation, like all meditation, is not fixed upon a point. In meditation, the *chitta* or mind is not fixed upon one thing; there is movement! The movement may be limited to the extent that the meditation is upon the *sushumna* only, but there is no limit on the movement of consciousness within that field. The only thing limited is the field of attention.

The *kechari-mudra* is very popular. It is said to promote concentration. It involves rolling the tongue back so that it touches the posterior nares. This may not be easy to do. Other yoga texts like the *Gerandha Samhita* suggest the *nabho-mudra* where the tongue is turned back onto the palate towards the uvula as far as it will go. It is believed that mental agitation ceases when the tip of the tongue is turned up and back. *Nabho-mudra* is considered a substitute for *kechari-mudra*.

Yoni-mudra is excellent for meditation upon the *chakras* because it completely blocks out or seals off all distractions. It gets its name *yoni,* meaning "uterus", because like the baby in the uterus, the practitioner has no external contact with the world and, therefore, no externalisation of consciousness. The physical posture that is recommended is *siddhasana* because it is considered the best for sealing off the lower apertures. If *siddhasana* is not possible, try *padmasana.*

The yogi then seals all the upper apertures. First, the ear holes are closed by putting the thumbs in the ears. Keep your back straight. Next close the eyelids, and place the tips of the index fingers on them. If the eyeballs feel disturbed by the pressure of the finger on the eyelids, try drawing the eyelid down with the index fingers so that the only place where the fingers apply pressure is just below the eyes (at the cheekbone). The middle fingers push in on the nostrils. The ring fingers rest on the upper lip, while the little fingers rest under the lower lip. Each elbow should be pointed outwards: the right at a ninety- degree angle to your right side, and the left elbow at a ninety-degree angle to your left side. Keep them in this position throughout, i.e., do not let them drop. You are allowed to prop them up with something, if necessary.

Serious practitioners use a t-shaped stick called a *yoga-danda*, which keeps the elbows stationary. By putting pressure on the armpit, the *yoga-danda* is also supposed to change the flow of energy in the *nadis*. This would be desirable if the alteration of the flow of energy, which in a healthy person has its own natural rhythm of alternation, had somehow become restricted due to some disturbance somewhere in the body-mind complex. If this were to happen, the normal regulation of energy from one side of the body to the other would be very sluggish and the flow on one side would dominate for quite longer than usual. To help counter this, the *yoga-danda* is placed under the armpit on the side in which the energy flow is dominant. If the energy flow is dominant on the left (the *ida*), the yogi places the *yoga-danda* under the armpit on the left side, and the flow will begin to shift, and will eventually start flowing in the *pingala nadi* on the right side.

There are two variations in the technique of breathing while doing the *Yoni Mudra*. The first is simply to stop pinching the nostrils with your middle fingers when you wish to breathe in and out. In the other procedure, the nostrils are held tightly shut. The ring and little fingers stay put also, but the lips open as if you are pouting, or, as if you are about to whistle. Breathing through the mouth is recommended in the *Gerandha Samhita*, and is known as *Kaki Mudra*. Some teachers like Swami Sivananda recommend breathing through the nose. The practitioner should choose the most convenient method.

In *Yoni Mudra*, the yogis do not suggest any ratio for the inhalation-retention-exhalation of the breath. Don't be concerned with how long you prolong the inhalation-exhalation. As with most of the yoga practices, here the retention of the breath is important. Hold the breath for as long as you like. And, as you hold the breath, concentrate and visualise each *chakra* singularly, and for some time, visualising, for example, the four-petalled *chakra* with the yellow square at the place where the body touches the ground. You visualise the two deities, and everything else in the descriptions that you have been given, and repeat the mantra, etc., until you are one with that earth centre, and become absorbed in it. The consciousness then moves up to the next centre.

In *chakra* meditation, yogis have experienced different "sounds". In the *Gerandha Samhita*, the seven main yoga practices were given to enable the student to hear the "inner sounds". Mudra is one of seven practices that yogis employ in order to aid the hearing of these inner sounds.

In *Yoni Mudra* yogis not only visualise each one of the *chakras*, but also listen intently to inner sounds or what is popularly called "the mystic sounds". The yoga texts say that if you are right-handed, you will hear these sounds in your right ear and if you are left-handed, you will hear these sounds in your left ear.

Another Mudra practice that the yoga texts also recommend for the hearing of the inner sounds is *Sambhavi Mudra*. Like *Yoni Mudra*, it is also more of a spiritual practice than a physical exercise. Yoga texts mention that you should sit in *siddhasana*, and close your ears with the thumbs (as in the *Yoni Mudra*). Although the eyes are kept open in *Sambhavi Mudra,* the practitioner is supposed to "look without wanting to see anything". The eyes remain open, but the attention is within. The practice is a 'seal' in that consciousness is prevented from externalising which, in turn, prevents the arousal of objects from within itself. When all externalisation ceases, there is the experience of great inner joy. This is the reason that some yogis, including the Tibetans, call Mudra the "fountain of joy".

Since these Mudras are intended for use in *chakra* meditation, it is recommended that they not be combined with other types of meditation. That will compromise their effectiveness. For the committed student or practitioner, there are numerous purificatory practices, numerous *pranayama* practices, numerous *asanas*, numerous Mudras, all providing varied opportunities for meditation and self-discovery.

We have skimmed the surface obviously considering the limitations of condensing a topic that is ancient, rich and profound in its every fold to mere words. The great masters have spent lifetimes in the discovery of Mudras, and with every passing day a little more is added to the vast repertoire of knowledge on the subject. Just imagine: a seemingly innocuous gesture of the fingers, a little prayer, a touch of visualisation and pronto you are transported to a new consciousness. The more one delves into the subject, the less one knows. And learning all about it will take as much time as it took for creation to manifest itself in all its splendour.

Preferable Accompaniments: Music and Colour

An environment that is conducive is a great catalyst in any meaningful activity. The right surroundings, good music, diet, colours, fragrances and so many other compatible factors usher quality moments to the seeker. These moments can be infinite and open windows of great joy and enchantment to the genuine believer. He/she will be seized with an inexplicable ecstasy that will consume his every pore.

The right music has a calming effect. Even in hospitals, music accompanies surgery these days. Its therapeutic effects, even on plants and animals, have been well documented, and its accompaniment with Mudras transports the practitioner into a state of deep relaxation.

However, the choice of music remains personal though classical music, solo concerts, instrumental music and airy sounds have been found to be conducive to the right mood elevation necessary for the spiritual journey. Soft music abets a softer mood and hard, blaring music can move inherent aggression into fifth gear.

Along with music, colours too play an important part. There is no rule of thumb and there are no 'bad' colours and 'good' colours. The use of colours is also subjective and is dependent on personal taste, moods, imagery, the way we feel about ourselves, our personal evolution and development, and so many other factors.

Research into colours has thrown up some interesting conclusions on how they influence us. Red is supposed to improve circulation, orange helps as a mood elevator, yellow stimulates digestion, violet is the colour of transformation, brown is stable, black protects, green regenerates, blue is calming, and white contains all the colours and stands for purity.

So don't ever underestimate the power of compatible music and colour. For growth of any kind, the right ambience is vital. In the big cities of today, yoga, meditation and other self-healing techniques have staged a fashionable comeback. The stressed-out executive has realised that money and the gizmos it affords can't keep him sane or healthy. So there are retreats, conclaves, resorts, communes, even little corners in crowded homes that provide a little slice of private space for the soul seeker.

Alternate therapies, self-healing, various types of realisations and actualisations are falling over each other in a hurry as the human experience has not only magnified but also been blister packed into a tiny time capsule. Every generation gets smarter, and burnout is early. So all forms of healing have been culled out of the past with a vengeance as the neo-man in the Aquarian Age is hooking up to *Nirvana* faster than his coffee turning black.

The Meaning of "Namaste"

The gesture of *Namaste* is essentially Indian and therefore ancient. It is an integral part of Indian culture; its very essence is encapsulated in the hold of both palms held erect together in front of the bosom in greeting. It is used always, is not dependent on occasion, and is quintessentially Indian. In that simple gesture lies the timelessness of India, the mother culture of the world. If any one gesture were to be recognised as representative of Brand India, there is no doubt it is the simple, humble and overpoweringly significant *Namaste*. It is also one of our largest exports.

Atmanjali Mudra

Namaste represents the belief that there is a Divine spark within each of us that is located in the heart *chakra*. The gesture is an acknowledgment of the soul in one by the soul in another. In a literal translation, "*Nama*" means *bow*, "*as*" means *I*, and "*te*" means *you*. Therefore, *Namaste* means, "bow me you" or "I bow to you".

To perform *Namaste*, we place the hands together at the heart *chakra*, close the eyes, and bow the head. It can also be done by placing the hands together in front of the third eye, bowing the head, and then bringing the hands down to the heart. This is an especially deep form of respect.

For a teacher and student, *Namaste* allows two individuals to come together energetically to a place of connection and timelessness, free from the bonds of ego-connection. In yoga class, *Namaste* should ideally be done at the beginning and at the end of class. But *Namaste* needs no occasion. It can be performed anywhere, anytime, any place, without ritual or preconditions. It is an instinctive, unconditional thanksgiving to creation.

Anjali Mudra

Anjali means "offering", and *Anjali Mudra* is often accompanied by the word *Namaste*. This gesture is also found within certain asanas – in *Tadasana* (Mountain Pose), before you begin *Sun Salutations*, or in balance poses such as *Vrksasana* (Tree Pose). This sacred hand position is found throughout Asia.

Bowing and bringing the hands together in front of another person is sometimes mistakenly interpreted as a sign of submission. Many so-called "modern" men and women find doing *Namaste* uncomfortable. These days, in urban India, with the erosion of our traditions, and the continuous assault of western influences, it is not hip and 'cool' to do *Namaste* anymore. It is not considered trendy and is supposed to be old-fashioned. But that's only because generation next doesn't understand the beauty of this gesture, which positions us right at the core of our being. The handshake has taken over as the urbane gesture of welcome, sadly devoid of meaning when compared to the rich cultural tradition of the *Namaste*.

Anjali Mudra is one of thousands of types of Mudras that are used in Hindu rituals, classical dance, and yoga. As the consummate Indian greeting, like a sacred hello, *Namaste* is often translated as "I bow to the divinity within you from the divinity within me". This salutation is at the essence of the yogic practice of seeing the Divine within all of creation. Hence, this gesture is offered equally to temple deities, teachers, family, friends, strangers, and before sacred rivers and trees.

As you bring your hands together at your centre, you are literally connecting the right and left hemispheres of your brain. This is the yogic process of unification, the yoking of our active and receptive natures. In the yogic view of the body, the energetic or spiritual heart is visualised as a lotus at the centre of the chest. *Anjali Mudra* nourishes this lotus heart with awareness, gently encouraging it to open as water and light do a flower.

Begin the Mudra by getting into a comfortable sitting position like *Sukhasana* (Easy Pose). Lengthen your spine out of your pelvis and extend the back of your neck by dropping your chin slightly in. Now, with open palms, slowly draw your hands together at the centre of your chest as if to gather all your resources into your heart.

Repeat that movement several times, contemplating your own metaphors for bringing the right and left side of yourself – masculine and feminine, logic and intuition, strength and tenderness – into wholeness.

Now, to reveal how potent the placement of your hands at your heart can be, try shifting your hands to one side or the other of your midline and pause there for a moment. Don't you feel slightly off balance as though the centre of gravity had shifted? Now shift back to the centre and notice how satisfying the centre line is, like a magnet pulling you into your core. Gently touch your thumbs into your sternum (the bony plate at the centre of the rib cage) as if you were ringing the bell to open the door to your heart. Broaden your shoulder blades to spread your chest open from the inside. Feel space under your armpits as you bring your elbows into alignment with your wrists. Stay here for some time and take in your experience. There may be shifts in mood and consciousness.

Next, imagine that you are beginning your yoga practice – or any activity in which you want to be centred and conscious of how your inner state will affect the outcome of your experience. Take *Anjali Mudra* again, but this time slightly part your palms as if to make a cup, so that your hands resemble the bud of a lotus flower. Depending on your spiritual orientation, you can metaphorically plant a seed prayer, affirmation, or quality such as "peace", "clarity", or "vitality" within your *Anjali Mudra.* Drop your chin towards your chest and awaken a sense of humility and awe with which to begin your practice, as if waiting to receive a blessing of good things to come. It is important that this *anjali* or offering be true to your Self as that will be the most effective and uplifting for you. Align your mind (awareness), feeling (heart), and actions (body) within this gesture. When you feel your invocation is complete, draw your fingertips to the centre of your forehead, *ajna chakra*, and pause there feeling the calming effect of your touch. Bring your hands back to your centre to ground your intention within your heart.

Now start whatever you have to. You will feel joyous, connected and in the present. The moment will resonate with peace and meaning. Notice how much easier it is to be present and joyous with whatever you are doing. *Anjali Mudra* can also be used within the Sun Salutations and many other *asanas* as a way to come back to and maintain your centre. When your hands come together overhead in *Virabhadrasana* I (Warrior I) or in Tree Pose, this is still *Anjali Mudra*. Consciously connecting this upward movement of your hands through an invisible line of energy to your heart will help your posture and your inner attitude. *Anjali Mudra* can be done any time and at the beginning and end of any task that is important to you.

In daily life, this prayerful gesture can be used as a way of bridging inner and outer experience, when saying grace before meals, communicating our truth within a relationship, or as a means of cooling the fires of stress when feeling rushed or reactionary. *Anjali Mudra* is an age-old means of helping human beings to remember the gift of life and to use it wisely. This Mudra seems ancient, almost as old as the beginning of time. It is rich in flavour, meaning and substance. In a moment of simplicity, we are transported to eternity through the *Anjali Mudra*.

Mudras in the Martial Arts

L ike different forms of yoga, Mudras are widely used in the combative arts. Anything that can empower, anything that can solidify the body and mind, is used in all forms of self-enhancement, whatever the origin and without prejudice.

Reliable sources point out that the origin of Mudras date to esoteric Buddhism, particularly the *Tendai* and *Shingon* sects. In ancient times, Mudras in martial arts were supposed to generate spiritual focus and power, which helped the student immensely.

But today, with modern concepts and newer methods of training, Mudras are not in vogue. Like several ancient traditions, they have been placed squarely in the tomes of history. So Mudras, *Mantras* (chanting or words of power), and *Mandalas* (inscriptions, paintings or scrolls that can create spiritual energy), so much a part of the young martial artist's curriculum once upon a time, are now, at best, mere memory. But if the teacher is a purist, the influence of Mudras in his teaching will not be lost even today.

Mudras give the *katas* in martial arts a definite edge. The use of Mudras sometimes explains some odd movements in the middle of a *kata*, which doesn't account for its necessity in a particular fighting technique. There are magical and secretive explanations to Mudras used in the martial arts, which can be difficult to comprehend even for the martial artist. Take a simple gesture of returning the sword to the scabbard. Even here there is a subtle play of fingers. This is not an affectation of a particular style but the secret inscription of a Mudra with the fingers to finish the combat, to ward off evil spirits, and to offer prayers to the dead.

Mudras have often been used in combination with various rituals and chants in the martial arts. One common Mudra is that of the "knife hand", or *shuto*. The first two fingers are extended while the thumb and other fingers are clenched. On closer examination, this movement may be found subtly hidden in some works belonging to the old schools of martial arts or in statues of divine Buddhist beings. This represents the sword of enlightenment, which cuts away all delusions. Sometimes, the tips of the extended fingers are grasped in the fist of the other hand. There is a symbolic meaning for this too.

Another common Mudra is the *kuji no in*, or the nine hand signs used in conjunction with nine words of power that generates spiritual strength for the user. The two hands weave a series of nine gestures made in conjunction with nine words derived from Sanskrit.

Other than seeing a *mikkyo* priest or a *koryu* practitioner perform a Mudra, you may even see it in a cheesy Japanese *ninja* movie or the like, because *ninjas* were like magicians in the eyes of the common people.

There are tales, even in modern historical times, of some adepts who could shout *(kiai)* and knock down birds in flight. Then the mystical *kiaijutsu* master could shout again and awaken the birds from their stupor. *Tai chi chuan* masters, it is said, could and, presumably, can still repel attackers with their spiritual *chi* energy. Mudra, like these fantastic powers, are found in many *koryu* as part of their esoteric nature.

Mudra is a Sanskrit word meaning *sign* or *seal*. It is a gesture or position, usually of the hands, that locks and guides energy flow and reflexes to the brain. By curling, crossing, stretching and touching the fingers and hands, we can "talk" to the body and mind as each area of the hand corresponds to a certain part of the mind or body.

From the little finger to the thumb: each finger represents earth, metal, fire, wood, and water, respectively. The entire universe lies within your ten fingers and it is also said that there is an infinite number of Mudras even though we only have 10 fingers. Mudras can be used both for meditation and/or healing.

Mudras can have several meanings. It can be a mere gesture, a position of the hands, a symbol, eye positions, body postures, even breathing techniques. In *Hatha Yoga,* with the focus on physical exercises, cleansing and breathing, there are 25 Mudras. In *Kundalini Yoga,* which aims to optimise spiritual strength, the hand Mudras are used for greater effect.

The primary goal of yoga is the oneness of humanity with cosmic consciousness. The thumb is symbolic of cosmic consciousness and the index finger of individual consciousness. The index finger represents inspiration and the thumb stands for intuition. When the tips of both fingers meet, the connection is complete – intuition and inspiration form a closed unity.

Origins

The origin of Mudras is still shrouded in mystery. They are found throughout the world and have been in use for aeons. Mudras are found in everyday life, in religion, dance, art, and even in Tantra. Mudras are extremely important in Hindu and Buddhist iconography. Their significance is both exoteric and esoteric. They are also a useful aid to identification of Buddhas, Bodhisattvas and deities.

The following are some of the most common Mudras:

❑ *Abhaya Mudra*: Mudra of blessing or protection. Right

hand, held at shoulder level, pointed upwards with the palm facing outwards.

- ❑ *Anjali Mudra*: Mudra of greeting, gesture of respect and, of course, prayer. Palms together at the level of the heart, with fingertips pointed upwards.

- ❑ *Vitarka Mudra*: Teaching Mudra. Held at chest level, the right hand faces outwards. The thumb and forefinger form a circle. Pointing downwards, the left hand faces outwards or lies palm up in the lap.

- ❑ *Varada Mudra*: Mudra of giving, or generosity. Pointed downwards, the palm of the right hand faces out.

- ❑ *Dharmachakra Mudra*: Mudra of turning the wheel of the *Dharma* (teaching). Hands held level with the heart, the thumbs and forefingers of each hand form circles that touch one another. The left hand faces inwards, the right hand out.

- ❑ *Bhumisparsha Mudra:* Earth-touching (also called 'earth-witness') Mudra. The left hand rests in the lap with the palm facing upwards. The right hand rests palm down on the right knee with fingers pointing towards the earth.

- ❑ *Dhyani Mudra*: The meditation Mudra. The back of one hand (usually the right) rests on the upturned palm of the other, with the tips of the thumbs lightly touching. There are several variations on this.

Buddhas, Bodhisattvas, Hindu Deities and Mudras

We take a break from the healing aspects of Mudras and look at the pantheon of gods and goddesses around the world in their various incarnations and Mudras. Beliefs are subjective and are dependent on a variety of factors, which can range from the topography and climate to sheer economics and food habits. Most gods and goddesses in the East have been crafted with great skill, creativity and imagination. Even today they dazzle the most brilliant minds by the forms, colours and Mudras they inhabit to depict the feelings, emotions and aspirations that they do.

It is no coincidence that our deities are in various Mudras. As we continue with the book, we will realise that the Mudras chosen by the embodiments of divinity are very specialised. Each Mudra reflects a definite standpoint predetermined by the deity. So all this is not new. Mudras are ancient. Long before we touched water on Mars, our ancestors knew about the enormous power in our fingers. And then the relevant Mudra was transposed to the deity of choice based on the role he or she was expected to play in our lives.

Buddhas

In the various schools of *Mahayana* (the 'greater vehicle') Buddhism (which includes Tibetan Buddhism, Chinese

Ch'an and Japanese Zen, etc.) most of the Buddhas mentioned below are recognised. *Theravada* (or *Hinayana*, 'the lesser vehicle', the Buddhism of Sri Lanka, Thailand and Burma) Buddhism just recognises Sakyamuni (and perhaps Maitreya and a few others) and so Amoghashiddhi will be referred to as Sakyamuni, with hands in *Abhaya Mudra*, etc., rather than Amoghashiddhi. Buddhism in Nepal has a tendency to mix and recognise both Buddhas and Hindu deities.

The Five Dhyani Buddhas

The *Five Dhyani Buddhas* are celestial Buddhas visualised during meditation, and considered to be great healers of the mind and soul. They are not historical figures, like Gautama (Sakyamuni) Buddha, but transcendent beings who symbolise universal divine principles or forces.

Akshobhya

Akshobhya is regarded as the second *Dhyani* Buddha by the Nepali Buddhists. He sits in the Vajraparyanka pose and his right hand is in the Bhumisparsha (earth-touching) Mudra, calling the earth for witness (*Sakyamuni* usually adopts the same pose). He represents the primordial cosmic element of *Vijnana* (consciousness). His left hand rests in his lap, while the right rests on his right knee with the tips of the middle fingers touching the ground with the palm facing inwards. His vehicle is a pair of elephants, and his symbol is the *vajra* (thunderbolt). His female counterpart is *Locana*.

Amitabha Buddha

Amitabha is the most ancient Buddha among the *Dhyani* Buddhas. He is said to reside in the *Sukhabati* heaven in peaceful meditation. He represents the cosmic element of *Sanjna* (name). His vehicle is a peacock. He sits in the full-lotus posture, right leg over left, with his palms folded face up, the right on top of the left, on his lap in *Samadhi*

Mudra. His female counterpart is *Pandara*. Amitabha denotes 'boundless light' or the incomprehensible.

Amoghashiddhi Buddha

Amoghashiddhi is the fifth *Dhyani* Buddha. He sits in the full-lotus posture, left leg over the right, with his left hand open, palm facing upwards, on his lap, and the right in the *Abhaya Mudra*. He represents the cosmic element of *Samskara* (the birth and death cycle). His colour is green and his symbol is the *viswa vajra* or double thunderbolt. He is the embodiment of the rainy season. His vehicle is *Garuda*.

Ratna Sambhav Buddha

Ratna Sambhav is regarded as the third *Dhyani* Buddha. His symbol is the jewel and his hands are in the *Varada* (gift-bestowing) *Mudra*. He represents the cosmic element of *Vedana* (sensation). His colour is yellow. His female counterpart is *Mamaki*.

Vairochana Buddha

Vairochana is regarded as the first *Dhyani* Buddha by the Nepali Buddhists. He represents the cosmic element of *Rupa* (form). His colour is white, and his two hands are held against the chest with the tips of the thumbs and forefingers of each hand united, in the *Dharmachakra* (preaching) *Mudra*. His female counterpart is *Vajradhatviswari*.

Bhaisajya Buddha

Bhaisajya (known as the medicine or healing Buddha) is said to dispense spiritual medicine when properly worshipped. He wears a monastic robe and is seated with legs crossed. His left hand, lying on his lap in the meditation Mudra, usually holds a medicine bowl, while the right hand, in the charity mudra, holds either a branch with fruit, or the fruit alone, of *myrobalan,* a medicinal plant found in India.

Hotei (also Budai, or The Laughing Buddha)

The Japanese name for the Chinese Zen Master Poe-Tai Hoshang (10th to 11th century). Fat, grotesque and lovable, he symbolises the state of detached bliss, which belongs to those who realise their Buddha Nature, or the Buddha within. He is loved the world over and worshipped by many as the God of Good Fortune (he is also regarded by some as a form of *Maitreya*).

Maitreya Buddha

The Buddha of the future. Usually shown standing and holding a lotus stalk in his right hand, or seated with legs either dangling or left leg down with right leg on left thigh, with hands in *Dharmachakra* (teaching) *Mudra*.

Sakyamuni Buddha

Gautama Buddha is believed to have had 550 incarnations. To distinguish him from all other Buddhas, he is known as Sakyamuni (Sage of the Sakya Clan). He was born in 563 BC in Lumbini, Nepal, the son of King Suddhodana and Queen Mayadevi. He attained enlightenment after six years of meditation and fasting. He died aged 80 in Kushinagara. Usually shown seated in *padmasana* (lotus posture) with right hand in *Bhumisparsha* (earth-touching) *Mudra*. Sometimes shown standing with right hand in *Abhaya* (protecting) *Mudra*.

Bodhisattvas

Amitayus

Amitayus is the name given to Amitabha in his character as bestower of longevity. He is richly clad and wears the 13 ornaments. His hair is painted blue and may either be coiled or left lose to fall to his elbows. He is seated in full-lotus posture and his hands lie on his lap in the *Dhyani Mudra*, holding the ambrosia vase, his special emblem.

Avalokiteswara

The Bodhisattva of compassion, protector from danger. His invocation is *Om Mani Padme Hum* (hail the jewel in the lotus). He is usually depicted with many (supposedly 1000) arms and several (supposedly 11) heads. One right hand is usually in the *Abhaya* (protection) *Mudra*. The Dalai Lama is said to be an embodiment of *Avalokiteswara*.

Green Tara

Green Tara is regarded as the spiritual consort of Amoghashiddhi. Similar in appearance to White Tara, her left hand holds a half-closed lotus flower and her right leg is extended. She is supposed to be reincarnated in all good women.

4-armed Chenrezig

4-armed Chenrezig is a form of *Avalokiteswara*. He wears all sorts of ornaments, his colour is white. He has four arms and carries a rosary in one right hand and an open lotus flower in one left. The other two hands are raised to the chest with the palms joined in *Namaskar Mudra*, holding a round 'jewel' (a symbol of knowledge).

Manjushri

Manjushri is the Bodhisattva of divine wisdom. In Nepal he is regarded as the founder of Nepali civilisation and the creator of Kathmandu Valley. He carries the sword of wisdom and light in his right hand and the Prajnaparmita manuscript (the book of divine wisdom) in his left on a lotus blossom. His left hand is in the teaching *Jnana Mudra*.

Vajradhara

Adi Buddha is regarded as the highest deity of the Buddhist pantheon. When represented, he is given the name of *Vajradhara*. He wears jewels and ornaments and sits in the meditation posture. He carries the *vajra* (thunderbolt) in his right hand and the *ghanta* (bell) in his left, the two hands crossed against the chest in the *Vajrahunkara* Mudra.

Vajrasattva Buddha

Vajrasattva, the sixth *Dhyani* Buddha, is regarded by the Nepali Buddhists as the priest of the five *Dhyani* Buddhas. He wears all ornaments, a rich dress and a crown. He is white and sits cross-legged in the meditative pose. He carries the *vajra* (thunderbolt) in his right hand with palm upwards against the chest, and *ghanta* (bell) in the left hand resting on the left thigh.

White Tara

Tara is the female deity of the Buddhist Pantheon. White Tara was born from a tear of the Bodhisattva of compassion, *Avalokiteswara*. Tara is believed to protect human beings while they are crossing the ocean of existence. White Tara is regarded as the consort of *Avalokiteswara*, sometimes of *Vairochana*. She is portrayed usually seated, dressed and crowned like a Bodhisattva. Sometimes she is regarded as *Satalochana* or seven-eyed Tara, and has extra eyes on her forehead, palm and feet, and a lotus flower on one or both of her shoulders. She is seated in full *Vajra* posture. Her right hand will be in boon-conferring posture, her left in the teaching Mudra, holding the stem of a lotus. She is wearing all sorts of precious ornaments and looks beautiful. The practice of White Tara is performed to prolong life and for healing purposes.

Kuanyin

The Chinese female form of the Bodhisattva of Compassion, *Avalokiteswara*, referred to as 'The Goddess of Mercy', called *Kannon* (or *Kanzeon Bosatsu*) in Japan. She usually carries a vase containing the nectar of compassion, and perhaps a flywhisk, which represents obedience to the Buddhist Law and symbolises compassion. Sometimes she is represented holding her palms together in *Anjali Mudra*.

Others

Padmasambhava

A renowned and highly learned Tantric saint of Northern India, Padmasambhava went to Tibet at the invitation of the 8th century King Thi-Sron Detsan and remained there for 50 years, founding monasteries and teaching Tantra. He is represented seated on a lotus dais with the legs locked, the right hand holding the *vajra* and the left, lying in his lap, the *patra*. He holds his special symbol, the *khatvanga*, pressed against his breast with his left arm.

Je Tson-ka-pa

Je Tson-ka-pa was born in Tibet in the middle of the 14th century and it is said that the tree that overshadowed the house in which he was born had the imprint of a Buddha on its leaves. He was a Northern Buddhist reformer and founded the Gelugpa sect, which became very popular in Tibet and has remained the most important sect till the present day.

Hindu Deities

Bhairav

The wrathful, Tantric aspect of Shiva, Bhairav is portrayed as naked, black or blue, with long, unruly flaming hair and holding a sword in one hand and a wand with three skulls or a noose in the other. He often has a string of skulls round his neck and stands on a recumbent figure. Sometimes shown embraced by his consort, Kali (*Bhairav Shakti*).

Brahma

The lord of creation and the god of wisdom, he has four faces, representing the four qualities of the earth, directed in four directions. He holds in his hands the Vedas (ancient book of wisdom and learning), a string of pearls for counting time, and a sacrificial spoon symbolic of spiritual nature. The fourth hand is usually raised in blessing. He also carries water in a *Kamandalu* (water pot), indicating that the universe has evolved from water.

Durga

A wrathful form of Parvati (consort of Shiva), Durga is represented with many arms with a weapon in each hand, shown sitting astride her mount, the lion, holding a sword, a club, a lotus flower and a dice. Her face always remains calm and gentle.

Ganesh

The elephant-headed god of wisdom and success, Ganesh is the defender and remover of obstacles, and has to be propitiated first before worship of other gods. He is one of the sons of Shiva and is known as *Siddhi Data*, or bestower of success in work. His elephant head is believed to be an emblem of wisdom and his mount (the shrew called *Mooshika*) an emblem of sagacity.

Kali

A wrathful form of Parvati (consort of Shiva), Kali is the goddess of mysteries. She is usually black or blue in colour and is represented unclothed except for a garland of severed heads, tongue protruding from her mouth.

Krishna

Like the Buddha, Krishna is considered to be a popular incarnation of Vishnu, symbolising many virtues, including love, devotion and joy. He is usually shown playing a flute, though often depicted as a little blue baby. His love for Radha is an allegory of the union of the individual soul with God.

Lakshmi

The goddess of wealth, and the wife of Vishnu, Lakshmi has four hands. The two prominent hands are in *Varada* and *Abhaya Mudra*. The other two hold a mirror and vermilion pot. She is often accompanied by two dwarfs.

Mahavira

Often and erroneously considered to be the founder of the Jain religion but actually the 24th *Tirthankara* (ford-maker), he is credited with the founding of modern Jainism, a religion that requires total commitment to non-violence (*ahimsa*). He was a contemporary of the Buddha and, in fact, Buddhism and Jainism have much in common. He was famed for his severe asceticism and complete rejection of the material world – he is said to have gone naked from the moment of his renunciation and to have had no connection with food, water, sleep or cleanliness.

Lord Mahavira in the Kevaljnana Mudra

Nataraj, the Lord of the Dance

The dance represents Shiva as the moving force of the universe and his five supernatural acts of creation, preservation, destruction, embodiment and release (of the souls of men from illusion – release being found in the fire of the cremation ground, here symbolised by the ring of flames around the dancer). Shiva is caught in mid-dance with one foot on a demon, the other poised for the next step. His hair flying out at the sides, he holds the hour-glass-shaped drum (representing the five rhythms of manifestation) and the ashes of fire with which he destroys the universe.

Saraswati

The goddess of learning, music and poetry, Saraswati is believed to confer wisdom and learning on those who worship her (she is revered by Hindus and Buddhists). She is the consort of Brahma and is generally represented holding a *Vina* (stringed musical instrument). Her colour is white and her mount a peacock.

Shiva

The god of destruction and regeneration in the Hindu pantheon, Shiva has many forms including: Shiva as a meditating ascetic, Nataraj – Lord of the Dance, Bhairav – Shiva in his wrathful aspect, the androgynous Ardhanari – half man, half woman, and in various forms with his consort Parvati/Uma/Durga/Kali. He usually holds a trident and a small drum, and the divine bull, Nandi, serves as his vehicle. He is the father of Ganesh.

Vishnu

The preserver and protector – popular because of his compassionate nature, worshipped either singly or with his consort Lakshmi (goddess of wealth). He is usually shown standing upright with four arms, one holding a wheel (*chakra*), another a mace or club (*gada*), another a conch shell (*shankh*) and the last a lotus bud (*padma*). He also wears a diadem (*kirit*) on his head and stands on a lotus pedestal. Krishna, Rama and Sakyamuni Buddha are said to be incarnations of Vishnu.

How to do a Mudra

Mudras are easy to do. Their effects are accentuated when combined with Reiki. The practitioner can then feel the energy flow strongly. There are no hard and fast rules though. But certain guidelines will help.

Start each Mudra session by "washing" your hands (rub your hands against each other about 10 times, hold hands before your *Navel Chakra*) this will help energy to flow in your hands. If you have Reiki II you can draw the *Power symbol* and the *Mental/Emotional symbol* over your hands (or any other symbol that you prefer).

There are several Mudras we will touch on as you progress with the book. A rule of thumb: When fingers touch the pressure exerted should always be very light and the hands should be relaxed.

Mudras can be done in any position. One can be seated, standing, lying down and even walking. The body should be loose and relaxed and centred. It is important not to be tense because that will hinder the flow of energy. Mudras are meant to loosen up, to travel into the consciousness and heal.

If you are seated, sit with your back straight, either with legs crossed or on a straight-backed chair. Put your fingers together as described in each Mudra. Just exert that much pressure to feel the flow of energy.

Mudras can be practised at any time and in any place. But it does help if one is in a good mood and in the right ambience. Then there will be no blocks to the easy flow of energy. Several serious practitioners do their Mudra ritual a few minutes before falling asleep and a few minutes before getting out of bed. But that is not really important. You can do them any time. Conversely, there are also several serious practitioners who do the Mudras at different times.

Go slow with the Mudras. Don't rush them. Try a few with patience. Do them slowly. Don't rush through a whole lot of them. It is easy to do that. You have the book in front of you with the instructions and the diagrams and it is very tempting to run through the whole lot of them as though it were a military exercise. But that is exactly what you shouldn't do.

Feel the Mudras work inside you. Don't expect miracles and then get disappointed when nothing happens. The changes that you will experience will be holistic. As your mind heals, the body will respond and you will begin to feel better and better. Many problems of the mind are manifested in the body. For them to heal, the mind will have to lead the way and that may take time. Hold on. Don't give up. The mind will heal slowly but surely and you will experience many wondrous feelings of joy and elation and finally the recovery will be complete and long lasting. The body also falls ill whenever the mind goes through turmoil and so different sets of Mudras may be needed at different times of one's life.

Soon, with the continuous practise of Mudras, along with the visualisation and the affirmation, you will find that you have embarked on a whole new journey of self-discovery. There is *chakra* energy in use, mood lifts and a new sense of calm and healing. Finally, the practitioner is delivered from the mundane demands of ordinary living. Or rather, he copes effortlessly. What once seemed hopeless is now no longer a problem.

There are divergent views on how long a Mudra should be held. Some recommend holding one Mudra per day for 45 minutes. If that is too long a stretch, divide it into three periods of 15 minutes each. Others have their own opinions on this. But it is beneficial if there is some regularity to it, like a daily exercise or meal timings or medication or something which we do on a regular basis. It is a good idea to discontinue the Mudra when the effect is achieved. Initially, one may feel tiredness but that is a good sign. When you start feeling well and whole and good over a period of time, which can be quite relative, you will notice the Mudra working for you.

Correct breathing plays a vital role. When we exhale deeply we discharge not only carbon dioxide but also expended energy. Pause a little more after inhaling and exhaling. When you need to calm yourself, slow the breathing, and when you need to refresh yourself intensify it. Breath plays a very important role. When it is deep, slow and flowing, the breath has a calming and regenerative effect on the body.

Various Mudras

The Om Mudra

This is probably one of the most well-known Mudras and is very easy to do. Sit with a straight back. Create the sacred *Om Mudra* by connecting the index finger with the thumb on the same hand (both hands). The thumb is the gateway to Divine Will (represented by the *Crown Chakra*) and the index finger is the Ego (represented by the *Navel Chakra*). As you do this Mudra you can do an affirmation or just chant *Om* (pronounced *Aum*). If doing the affirmation, say to yourself when you breathe in: "I am one with the Universe" and as you breathe out: "The Universe and I are one". This mudra is very good when your life is in need of peace and tranquillity.

We elaborate on *chakras* later in the book. We have also elaborated on visualisation earlier in the book, which is necessary for optimising the feel good yearning. Make affirmations, positivity and the right visualisation a lifestyle and you will see the benefits over a period of time.

The Smiling Buddha Mudra

This has been made world famous in paintings and statues. This is a gesture and exercise of happiness as it opens the flow of energy to the heart. Almost every home has a statute of the Buddha seated. Observe it carefully and watch the Mudra. You will find the Buddha seated in different Mudras.

Sit comfortably either with crossed legs or on a straight backed chair. Bend ring and little fingers, pressing them down with the thumbs. Keep index and middle fingers straight (be comfortable, do not force the fingers straight), palms forward. Push elbows in towards the body (as far as it feels comfortable for you) and keep a 30-degree angle between the upper arms and the forearms. Keep the forearms parallel to each other.

Concentrate on your Third Eye and mentally chant (at the Third Eye) *Sa Ta Na Ma* (*Sa* – Infinity, *Ta* – Life, Existence, *Na* – Death, *Ma* – Rebirth, Light). It can be done without the chant but try to at least concentrate on your Third Eye. The focus is essential.

Keep elbows in towards your body and your chest out (straight back). Continue for about 10 minutes, then inhale deeply, exhale, open and close the fists several times, and relax. Enjoy the experience! Fight worry, depression, impatience, anger, fear and other emotions. This Mudra can be done anywhere.

The fingers also correspond to emotions and the major organs. On the outside and inside of your fingers run the meridians with several acupuncture points located in them. By pressing or squeezing the sides of the fingers, according to your needs, you can affect both the emotion and the corresponding organ. This is called acupressure. Later in the book, we look at the fingers and their significance in Mudras and in maintaining a mind-body balance.

Ganesh Mudra

Ganesh, the elephant God, is universally acknowledged as the conqueror of obstacles. In this Mudra the left hand should be held in  front of the chest with the palm facing outward. Bend the fingers and grab the left hand with the right hand with the palm facing inward. Now both the hands are clasped. Exhale and vigorously pull the hands apart without releasing the grip. The hands are in front of the chest, and this action will tense the muscles of the upper arm and the chest area. Inhale and let go of the tension. Repeat six times. Change the hand positions and again do the exercise six times. Remain in silence for a while after this.

The exercise can also be done with one elbow pointing upwards and another pointing downwards. Do it once a day and the Mudra will strengthen the heart muscles and open the bronchial tubes and release tension. It also opens the fourth *chakra* and boosts confidence in the practitioner.

Ushas Mudra

This can be done while waking up in the morning. While in bed, place clasped hands at the back of the head. Inhale vigorously and deeply several times. Open 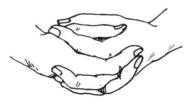 eyes and mouth wide and press elbows back into the pillow. The two hands should be clasped in such a way that the right thumb lies above the left pressing it lightly.

Women should place the right thumb between the left thumb and index finger, pressing on it with the left thumb. This can be done every day for about ten to fifteen minutes. This influences the second *chakra*, the centre of sexuality and creativity.

Pushan Mudra

In this Mudra, the tips of the right thumb, index finger and middle finger are on top of each other and the other two fingers, the ring finger and the little finger, are extended. Now with the left hand bring the tips of the thumb, middle finger and ring finger on top of each other with the index finger and the little finger extended.

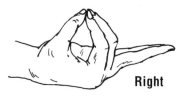

Right

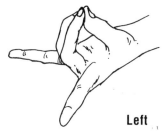

Left

This Mudra is dedicated to the sun god. It signifies accepting and receiving with one hand and letting go with the other. This Mudra helps with digestion and elimination.

It can also be done another way. The tips of the thumb, ring finger and little finger are on top of each other and the index finger and middle finger are extended. Now with the left hand connect the energies of the thumb, ring finger and little finger with the index finger and the middle finger extended.

This Mudra helps with elimination. It also stimulates the brain. These two Mudras can be practised four times a day for five minutes each.

Bronchial Mudra

As the name suggests, this Mudra is very good for respiratory problems. Do this with both hands. Place the little finger at the base of the thumb, the ring finger on the upper thumb joint and the middle finger on the top soft portion of the thumb. The index finger should be extended. This can be done for a few minutes everyday.

It can be done along with the *Asthma Mudra*, which is also done with both hands. Press together the fingernails of the middle fingers while keeping the other fingers extended. This is effective for asthma attacks. The *Bronchial* and the *Asthma Mudras* can be done for a few minutes one after the other until the breathing calms down. For prolonged treatment these two Mudras can be done five times every day for five minutes.

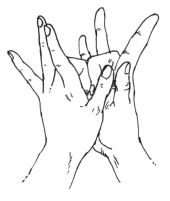

Pran Mudra

The *Pran Mudra* activates the root *chakra* and increases vitality. This can be done up to half an hour a day or three times a day for fifteen minutes. The tips of the thumb, ring finger and little finger are brought together while the index finger and the middle finger remain extended. This Mudra can be done with both hands.

Linga Mudra

In this Mudra place both palms together and clasp your fingers. One thumb remains upright and encircled by the thumb and index finger of the other hand. Keep both hands in front of the chest. This can be done three times a day for fifteen minutes. This Mudra boosts the body's immune system and loosens mucous that has collected in the lungs.

The *Linga Mudra* is believed to make the body more resistant to colds and chest infections. Those who habitually suffer from bad colds and incurable chest infections are advised to practise the *Linga Mudra*.

This Mudra generates heat in the body and "burns" away accumulated phlegm in the chest and makes the body more resilient, says Acharya Keshav Dev.

This Mudra is helpful in weight reduction too. However, because of the heat it generates, the Mudra can be taxing and can result in a feeling of lethargy. Weight-watchers who practise it must ensure that they consume 'cooling' foods like fruits or drink as much water as they can – at least eight glasses a day.

Apan Mudra

This is called the energy Mudra. The thumb, middle finger and ring finger are placed together and the index finger and little finger

are extended. This can be done for forty-five minutes or three times a day for fifteen minutes. This Mudra helps remove toxins from the body. This Mudra also has a balancing effect on the mind and helps develop inner balance and confidence.

Shankh Mudra

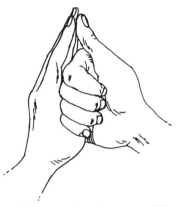

This Mudra is common in Hindu temples. The conch shell is blown during all rituals. In this Mudra, the positioning and clasping of the fingers simulate a conch shell. Encircle the thumb with the four fingers of the right hand. Touch the right thumb to the extended middle finger of the left hand. Now, together, the two hands resemble a conch shell. This can be done three times every day for fifteen minutes. Hold the hands in front of your sternum and chant *Om* with it.

This Mudra is very good for problems of the throat. Mudras are practised all over the world these days and have been incorporated in various schools of self-development and growth. The interesting part is that there is no escaping the Indian origins in most of them. The *Shankh Mudra* is an obvious example.

Surabhi Mudra

This can seem a bit complicated, almost like a puppet player's fingers in action. Here goes... The little finger of the left hand should touch the ring finger of the right hand and the little finger of the right hand should touch the ring finger of the left hand. The middle fingers of both hands should touch the index fingers of the other. The thumbs are extended. This Mudra can be done three times a day for fifteen minutes. It is supposed to be an effective tool against rheumatism.

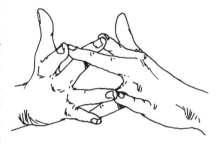

Vayu Mudra

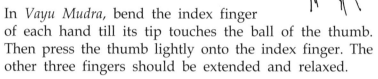

Vayu means wind and this Mudra is specifically aimed at eliminating flatulence. It is believed that it works almost immediately. But as soon as the problem is overcome, the Mudra should be discontinued. If the condition is chronic, the Mudra should be done thrice daily for fifteen minutes.

In *Vayu Mudra*, bend the index finger of each hand till its tip touches the ball of the thumb. Then press the thumb lightly onto the index finger. The other three fingers should be extended and relaxed.

Shunya Mudra

The middle finger should be bent until it touches the ball of the thumb. Then with the thumb lightly press down on the middle finger. The other fingers remain relaxed and extended. This should be done with both hands. This is especially good for ear and hearing problems and can be done three times daily for fifteen minutes.

Prithvi Mudra

The tip of the thumb should be placed on top of the ring finger with a little pressure. The other three fingers should be relaxed and extended. This can be done with both hands three times for about fifteen minutes a day.

This Mudra activates the root *chakra*, which houses our vital energy or elemental force. Vital energy is necessary

65

for successful living. Enormous vital energy is visible as is depleted vital energy. A good vital energy optimises the physical potential in a person who is then in a position to actualise both his physical and metaphysical goals. When there is a drop in it the person will feel physically and psychologically drained. Sick people are good examples of low vital energy. It is essential for a life of fulfilment to ward off energy deficits and the *Prithvi Mudra* is an ideal tool.

Varuna Mudra

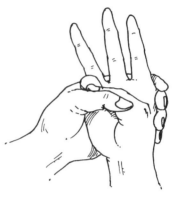

This Mudra is very good to get rid of the excess mucous that collects in the stomach or lungs. A mucous overload is normally associated with overstimulated nerves and by people who are too conscious of their responsibility. In their perception, they believe that they are saddled with every responsibility and it works on their bodies in the form of mucous accumulation.

In this Mudra bend the little finger of your right hand until the tip touches the ball of the right thumb. Then place the thumb of the right hand on it. With the left thumb press the little finger and thumb lightly while the left hand gently encircles the right hand from below, covering the back of the right palm.

Bhudi Mudra

More than eighty per cent of the human body is water and it is essential to maintain the right water balance in the body. The daily quota of water or liquids needed for a person is very individual and so no general rule can be drawn, but it is always better to drink a lot of glasses of water a day. Drinking more water won't harm, and it is always better to drink more than less. There is even the famous water cure, which insists on drinking loads of water at prescribed times of the day. But, whatever said and done, water is vital for the human body and there is no question of erring here.

Water has enormous energy. Its source or container is equally important. Various studies have shown that water molecules differ in energy from place to place, which is dependent on several factors like geography, climate, wars, pestilence, epidemics, poverty, suffering, happiness and so many other diverse reasons. Even the mood of the populace affects the quality of the water they drink. One can well imagine the quality of the water we drink in our cities, and that's why boiling and filtering it is so important. Waxing and waning of the moon also impacts the body's water flow. So the quality and quantity of water we consume over a lifetime is very significant.

The *Bhudi Mudra* helps maintain the fluid balance in the body. The tip of the thumb should be placed on the little finger while the other fingers remain relaxed and extended. Do this with each hand. This can be done three times a day for fifteen minutes.

Apan Vayu Mudra

This is called the Lifesaver and is the first aid for heart attacks. Mudras are excellent for health. There is no doubt about that. Every conceivable problem has a Mudra which enables a cure. *But **a note of** caution: If you are suffering* 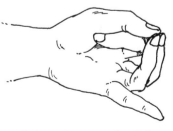 *from any disease, please heed the advice of your physician.* Please don't use Mudras as a substitute for medical treatment. This is particularly relevant when it comes to heart problems. Flatulence, earaches and a diminishing vital energy may not be instant killers but when it comes to sensitive organs like the heart, please don't rely solely on Mudras. Take your physician's advice and use the Mudra either as a preventive or a palliative in accompaniment with necessary medication.

A person who has developed heart trouble can check it by reducing the *vayu tatva* and *apan vayu* of his body. He can do this with the *Vayu* and *Apan Mudras*. In this Mudra, the index finger is brought down on the mound of the thumb, and the tips of the third and fourth fingers join the thumb. The little finger should be relaxed and extended. This can be done with each hand. This Mudra can be done three times a day for fifteen minutes or until the effect is felt.

This Mudra is supposed to have immediate effect in an emergency. It can also be used over a period of time to strengthen the heart. But, like we have cautioned, Mudras are NOT a substitute for medication.

Back Mudra

This is an excellent Mudra for backache. There are many reasons for backache. Stress is certainly one of them; in fact, stress is one of the prime causes. This Mudra is done with both hands. The thumb, middle finger and little finger of the right hand should touch, and the index finger and ring finger are relaxed and extended. In the left hand, place the thumb joint on the nail of the index finger. This can be done four times a day for four minutes.

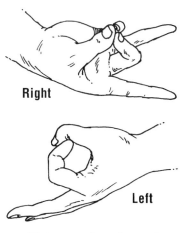

Right

Left

Kubera Mudra

This Mudra is dedicated to the god of wealth. In this you use three fingers – the tips of the thumb, index finger and middle finger are placed together. The other two fingers are bent and rest in the middle of the hand. This should be done with each hand.

This Mudra is quite remarkable. The three fingers here represent Mars, Jupiter and Saturn. Mars stands for forcefulness, Jupiter for resplendence and Saturn for its fixation on the essential. They are the thumb, middle finger and index finger respectively. When these three fingers close and is accompanied by intensity of thought, there is added strength.

This Mudra is not just for money. It can be used for several specific goals. If you need something badly, focus on it, visualise and do the *Kubera Mudra*. It is akin to calling forth renewed force. Formulate your desire in words and if it helps you and your world, ask what you need with positivity. Press the fingers together when you do this. Be affirmative, honest and positive. The *Kubera Mudra* decongests the frontal sinuses.

Kundalini Mudra

The traditionalists may argue this till the cows come home, but it has been proved medically and beyond all argument that good sex is essential for personal well-being. A sexual orgasm with a compatible partner is the closest an earthly act can take us to the inner sanctum of unadulterated joy. The moment of orgasm, as we all know, is a moment of sheer bliss, and the whiff of ecstasy stays with us long

after the act. Good, regular sex is dependent on several factors like good health, the right diet, freedom from stress and worry and, most important, an equally responsive partner. The right environment and other embellishments like good music, exciting fragrances etc. also help. But a lifetime of good loving is a lifetime of good health and happiness. Sexual desire should be indulged in. Period. With or without a partner. Sexual secretions have a cleansing function, and when you accept and yield to the body's needs, a glowing equanimity is all pervasive.

The *Kundalini Mudra* is associated with the sexual force that needs to be awakened. It is about the unification of the masculine and the feminine. In this Mudra, both the hands form a loose fist. Now extend the left index finger into the right fist from below and place it on the pad of the right thumb. The other fingers of the right hand cover the finger from above. It is like a loose and comfortable fleshy glove for the left index finger. Hold this Mudra as low as possible in front of the abdomen. Do this Mudra three times a day for fifteen minutes. Several schools of yoga and even the martial arts have recognised the immense power of the fountain of human sexual energy. It is the receptacle of regeneration and creativity; a force more powerful than nuclear fission. Optimising it is important for a life of fulfilment.

Ksepana Mudra

This Mudra stimulates elimination through the large intestine, skin and lungs. It helps release tensions of all kinds. Since we live in and around people all the time (there is no escaping that in overcrowded countries like India), we receive all kinds of energies, which can be negative and depleting. Privacy and solitude are essential. Without it we

can be robbed of essential energy, almost like being robbed of essential nutrients. We can become weak and our immune systems can get compromised with this continuous and unabated onslaught of negative energy. Despite this, not many people have the luxury of locking their rooms to the cacophony of the outside world in cities like Mumbai, which is forever running on an extra inoculation of adrenaline.

In this Mudra, the index fingers of both hands should be placed vertically against one another. The other fingers are clasped and interlocked with the fingers of one hand resting on the back of the other hand. The thumbs are crossed tight and placed against the hollow of the other thumb. The two touching index fingers should only have their tips meeting and there should be space between them. When you are seated, the index fingers should be pointed to the ground and when lying down they should point in the direction of the feet. The hands should be relaxed.

The *Ksepana Mudra* should be held for seven to fifteen breaths concentrating on the exhalation. Then the hands should be placed on the thighs with the palms turned upwards.

Rudra Mudra

The tips of the thumb, index finger and ring finger should be placed together. The middle and index fingers should be relaxed and extended. Do this with both hands  for about five minutes three to six times a day. The *Rudra Mudra* strengthens the earth element and its organs. It is a good antidote for weakness.

Garuda Mudra

The Garuda is the mystical bird that Lord Vishnu rides according to Hindu mythology. It is huge and powerful and is the king of the air. This Mudra activates the blood flow and the circulation. It also helps alleviate exhaustion.

In this Mudra clasp your thumbs and place your hands, the right on top of the left with the palms facing inwards, on your lower abdomen. Remain in this position for about ten breaths and then 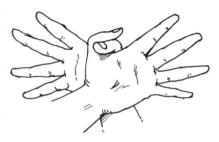 slide your hands to the navel. Remain there for another ten breaths. Then place your hands on the pit of the stomach and remain for another ten breaths. After this, place your left hand on the sternum, turn your hands in the direction of your shoulders and spread your fingers. Do this three times a day for four minutes.

Suchi Mudra

It is vital for health to have daily and good elimination. As you read on, you will realise that elimination is an important process in body-mind healing. It is not confined to the body alone, but cleansing is vital for the mind, soul and consciousness as well. The curative process is multi-pronged.

Prolonged constipation, apart from the discomfort, leads to several other medical problems. Intestinal cleaning is essential in yoga. Gastro and anorectal disorders are caused by stress, and if one doesn't have good daily elimination, the stress increases and can result in more medical and emotional problems; you then find yourself in the crux of a vicious cycle.

In this Mudra clench both fists and hold them in front of your chest. Inhale and stretch the right arm to the right and point the index finger upwards. Also, simultaneously, stretch the left arm to the left. Hold this for six breaths and return to the starting position. Repeat six times on both sides. If the constipation is serious, do this Mudra four times a day. For constipation that is not so severe, repeat six to twelve times in the morning and at noon.

Mushti Mudra

This Mudra too can be done in addition to the last one as it also promotes digestion and helps cure constipation. In this Mudra, bend the 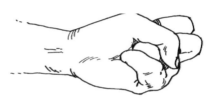 fingers inward and place the thumb over the ring fingers. Do this with each hand. Make them like fists. Do this Mudra three times a day for fifteen minutes.

Matangi Mudra

In this Mudra, fold your hands in front of your solar plexus. The fingers are clasped and the middle fingers are placed against one another with the fingers touching. They are not tightly held; there is space between them. Do this Mudra three times a day for four minutes. This Mudra strengthens the breathing impulse in the solar plexus.

Hakini Mudra

This is a very interesting and significant Mudra that can be practised anywhere, at any time. The fingertips of both hands should be placed together, the eyes directed upwards, the tip of the tongue should be placed on the gums while inhaling, and the tongue should fall again while exhaling. Then take a deep breath. This helps memory.

Unwittingly, this Mudra is quite popular. People inadvertently sit down in contemplation with both hands in front and the fingers touching at the tips as though in deep thought. This Mudra is good for the brain.

Tse Mudra

In this Mudra, place both hands on the thighs. Place the tip of the thumb on the root of the little finger. Encircle your thumbs with the other four fingers while slowly inhaling. Hold your breath for a few moments. Slowly exhale while holding in the abdominal wall. Then open hands and imagine all your worries leaving your body. Repeat this at least seven times. This is a good Mudra to handle depression.

Mahasirs Mudra

Here the tips of the thumb, index finger and middle finger touch each other. Extend the little finger and place the ring finger into the fold of the thumb. Do this with each hand three times a day for six minutes. This Mudra is good for headaches. It relieves tension and eliminates mucous congestion in the frontal sinuses.

Vajra Mudra

The three fingers – the middle finger, the ring finger and the little finger – should be bent and held together and the thumb pressed on to the side of

the middle fingernail. The index finger should be relaxed and extended. Do this with each hand three times a day for five minutes. This Mudra stimulates circulation.

Bhramara Mudra

In this Mudra, place the index finger in the fold of the thumb and the tip of the thumb on the side of the middle fingernail. The ring and little finger are relaxed and extended. Do

this with each hand. This can be done four times a day for seven minutes. This Mudra is good for allergies.

Uttarabodhi Mudra

Both hands should be placed in front of the solar plexus. The index fingers and thumbs of both hands should be laid on each other. The index fingers should point upwards and the thumb downwards. It can be held for any length of time. This Mudra refreshes the system and charges it with energy.

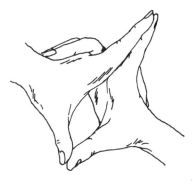

Detoxification Mudra

This Mudra is done with both hands. Place each thumb on the inner edge of the third joint of the ring finger. All the other fingers are relaxed and extended. This Mudra helps detoxify the system, which is so essential considering the muck it accumulates along the way, both physical and emotional. Detoxification is a comprehensive process of house cleaning and is necessary. The debris has to be given the sack and more room has to be created for greater positive energy, 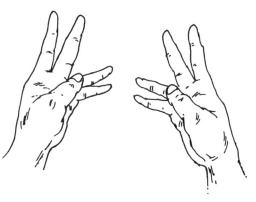 which can and should fill up the vacant spaces of the body and mind. Detoxification is a holistic process and has to be done with some regularity too.

The mind is a powerful ally in all this. I repeat the fact that the mind plays a vital role in the healing process. It is true with all the Mudras. You need to believe it works and you need to work on yourself to make positive changes happen. By simply learning the placing of the fingers and following easy-to-read instructions, don't expect the Mudras to effect miracle cures. There are several self-help books in the market and if a life change were so simple, the world would be a better place almost instantaneously. All one would have to do is to buy a book or visit a library and borrow one!

So whenever you practise these Mudras, get into yourself, enter the inner recesses of the private space that lives in all of us, ask for forgiveness, let the flood of healing overtake your being, focus the mind on your goal and do the Mudras. You are then most certainly on the first steps to recovery. It is a long process and must be persisted with. All inner journeys are much more profound, more significant and certainly more lasting than anything external. And when we work with the soul and with our consciousness, only persistence pays. So stick to it with doggedness and resolve.

Shakti Mudra

This Mudra has a calming effect and helps a person sleep. Place the ring and little fingers together; not tight but with a gap between them. The other two fingers are loosely bent over the thumbs which are  placed in the palm. Focus on breathing and slow down exhalation a bit. Do this Mudra three times a day for twelve minutes.

Maha Sacral Mudra

This Mudra is done with both hands. The ring fingers of both hands touch and the little fingers are on the thumbs. Hold this position for ten breaths. Now place the pads of the little fingers together and place the ring fingers on the thumbs. Hold for ten breaths. This Mudra can be done

three times a day for seven minutes. It is good for complaints of the lower abdomen. It can provide relief from pain during menstruation and provide relief from bladder and prostrate complaints as well.

Makara Mudra

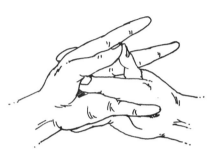

This is the crocodile Mudra. Place one hand inside the other and extend the thumb of the lower hand through the little finger and ring finger of the other and place it in the middle of the palm of the upper hand. This hand's thumb and the tip of the ring finger touch each other. It can be done three times a day for about ten minutes.

This Mudra activates kidney energy. It taps your reserves of strength.

Mukula Mudra

This seems very simple but is effective. Cup the hand. Place four fingers on the thumb. Your hand resembles a cone. Place it on that part of the body that needs more energy. This can be done with both hands five times a day for five minutes.

This Mudra is placed on the organ or body part that hurts or is tense. It is akin to directing energy to a specific part. Various organs are related to specific body parts. Place this Mudra at the right place and you feel instantly rejuvenated. It is like a sharp focus of healing energy, like a laser beam or a shaft of light, which is directed to the area of concern. It can be an effective healing tool.

Joint Mudra

As the name suggests, this Mudra is very good for the joints. This should be done with both hands. In the right hand put the thumb and ring finger together and in the left hand put the thumb and middle finger together. This Mudra can be done four times a day for fifteen minutes. It balances energy in the joints and is effective.

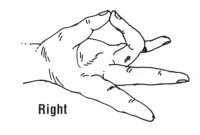

Right

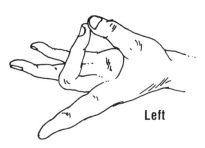

Left

Kalesvara Mudra

This Mudra calms the mind. It is powerful and can change character traits and eliminates addictive behaviour. It can be practiced for as long as twenty minutes a day. In this Mudra the middle fingers of both hands should touch at the tips. The first two joints of the index finger and the thumbs should touch. The little finger and the ring finger should be bent

inwards. The thumbs should be pointed towards the chest and the elbows spread out on the outside. Inhale and exhale slowly about ten times. Observe the breath and lengthen the pauses slowly after both inhalation and exhalation.

Shiva Linga

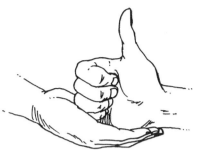

In Indian mythology, Shiva is the destroyer who makes way for new beginnings. Unless one dies, the other can't take birth. Nature, which epitomises life in its purest *avatar,* is replete with endings and beginnings. The *Shiva linga* or Shiva's phallus is the masculine force and the symbol of destruction and subsequent regeneration.

In this Mudra place the right hand with the thumb extended upward on top of the left hand. The left hand is like a tight bowl with the fingers held together and cupped. Both hands should be held at the abdomen and the elbows pointing outwards and slightly forward. The right hand will be like a fist with the thumb extending upward cradled in the cup of the left hand.

This Mudra can be done twice a day for four minutes or even longer. It regenerates and is a great healer as well.

Jnana Mudra and Chin Mudra

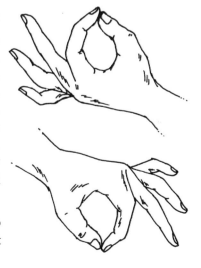

In this Mudra place the tip of the thumb on the tip of the index finger while the other fingers remain relaxed and extended. Do this with both hands and place them on the thigh in a relaxed position. When the fingers point upwards it is called *Jnana Mudra* and when they point downwards it is called *Chin Mudra.*

There are two ways to do this Mudra. In the first

method the tips of the thumb and the index finger touch each other. In the second method, the tip of the index finger touches the first thumb joint with light pressure. Both methods are different. The first is the passive receiving position, and the second one is an actively giving position.

These Mudras have a great effect on the person at several planes. This Mudra is found all over the world in different religions. It is very good for concentration and ensures the practitioner an uncluttered head.

Dynamic Mudra

Dynamic meditation as practised in the Osho ashram is all about energy and movement. (We touch on Osho, Tantra and Mudra later). As the name suggests, this meditation is dynamic. At the end of the session, the catharsis is complete. You feel like a new person. All the old baggage has been ejected and room has been made for new matter. It is like spring cleaning. Old leaves fade and fall off and new shoots emerge.

I mention this because Osho made dynamic meditation world famous and even management schools have adopted it after great scientific scrutiny. It has to be done to be believed. Lost, desperate, beaten people emerge winners after a session. It is a sight to behold. Fully grown men and women, successful by any yardstick but still searching for that something which gives life that finer edge, lost in the throes of dynamic meditation, yelling, screaming, jumping, journeying to exhaustion, and then crying like babies, spilling it all out of their systems like ejecting garbage or an old bag of bones. It's a truly cathartic process – effective and humbling for the practitioner and onlooker.

The cleansing process has been repeatedly stressed in every form of self-development. Even in *Vaastu* and *Feng Shui*, the importance of easy space for the *prana* to flow and be enriched is underscored. Clutter, in physical or metaphysical space, impedes the flow of energy. In our own lives, the inner clutter of everyday existence has to be expunged on a regular basis.

Much the same way, in Dynamic Mudra, the fingers move. Here I quote Gertrude Hirschi, world renowned yoga teacher, whose works on the subject are not only touched with erudition but with extreme compassion and empathy. Read her and you end up with your soul elevated and ready to touch the stars. In her words, in Dynamic Mudra, "During each exhalation, place one of your fingertips on the tip of your thumb; while inhaling, extend the fingers again. Speak a syllable mantra while doing this. Do this with each hand."

She then elaborates on the mantra to be used and how. "During *saaa*, press together the thumb and index finger; during *taaa*, use middle finger and thumb; during *naaa* use ring finger and thumb; during *maaa,* use little finger and thumb."

Gertrude adds, "When you do it the second time, press your fingernail instead of your fingertip with your thumb. During the third time, press your whole finger with the thumb. At the same time, press your fingertip into the palm of the hand."

This Mudra can be practised everyday for up to half an hour. While the Mudra is dynamic, keep the breathing slow. Inhale and exhale evenly. This Mudra relaxes the nerves.

Dhyani Mudra

This is a gesture of meditation. Both hands should be placed on the lap like bowls. The left hand lies in the right hand and the thumbs touch

each other. This is the classic meditation pose. The bowl shape made by the hands indicates that we are empty to receive new energy. This Mudra is like a submission. The practitioner humbly says that 'I am ready to receive'.

Lotus Mudra

Put your hands together, the fingers vertical, relaxed and spread out. The lower portion of the palms touch as well as the pads of the little fingers and thumbs. If the hands are closed, they resemble the bud of a lotus flower. When the hands open and the fingers spread out wide, it is akin to the lotus opening. After four deep breaths, close both hands back into a bud and place the fingernails of the fingers of both hands on top of each other. Then join the backs of the fingers, the backs of the hands and allow the hands to hang down for a while, all relaxed. Bring the hands back into the bud position and the open flower. Repeat several times.

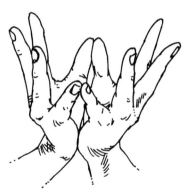

This Mudra belongs to the heart *chakra* and is the symbol for purity. It is good during times of loneliness and despair.

Mudra of The Inner Self

Hold the palms together, the tips of all the fingers touching. Keep the thumbs next to each other. The hands will appear like a pyramid on both sides, and between the tips of the thumbs and the tips of the other fingers that touch at the pads there is a tiny opening.

"This opening characterises the power of the heart through divine widsom. This opening is different for every human being," says Gertrude Hirschi. "Hold your hands in this position in front of your forehead and look through the opening, without blinking, as long as you can. Then lower your arms and hold the Mudra an inch or so beneath your chin for a while. Your hands will automatically be at the spot where the place of the soul lies. Now pay attention to your breathing. With every exaltation, very gently whisper 'Hoooo' and let yourself be carried through the little opening into infinity – into the great mystery. With this Mudra we enter and intone the world of the unfathomable, the Divine."

Bhumisparsha Mudra

While seated, the left hand is pointed down to the earth with the fingers touching the ground. The right hand points upwards like an open flower. This is the gesture of enlightenment.

Abhaya Mudra

In this Mudra raise the right hand to chest level with the palm facing forward, almost resembling a wave. Place the left hand on the left thigh, in the lap or on the heart. This Mudra promises freedom from fear.

Varada Mudra

Place the left hand forward and downward with the open palm facing outward. Place the right hand on the lap or thigh. This indicates forgiveness and is quite common in Hindu mythology.

Dharmachakra Mudra

This is very significant and symbolic of turning the wheel. In this Mudra raise both hands in front of the chest with the right hand higher than the left. Join the thumbs 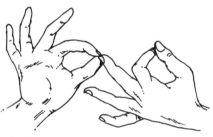 and index fingers of each hand. The palm of the left hand faces the heart and the back of the right hand faces the body. The left middle finger touches the place where the thumb and index finger of the right hand form a closed circle. While forming this Mudra, breathe deeply and slowly.

"The hands form two wheels," says Gertrude Hirschi. She adds that in Hindu mythology the wheel signifies completion. "The two wheels here indicate the teaching of reincarnation. The left middle finger (Saturn) represents the transition from this world into the next – from death and birth."

Naga Mudra

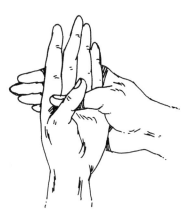

Also known as the Mudra of deep insight. In this Mudra, cross the hands in front of the chest and cross the thumbs over each other. The Naga Mudra is useful to solve everyday problems. It helps to work through obstacles that we encounter on the spiritual path.

Pushpaputa Mudra

Pushpa means flowers and this Mudra is a handful of flowers. Place both hands open and upwards against the thighs, relaxed and with the thumbs placed against the outer edge of the index finger. This Mudra is about openness and acceptance. The gesture itself resembles that emotion.

◇★◇

Fingers and Mudras

Mudras are all about the fingers, and each finger is packed with nerve endings, energy and a meaning all its own. The correct play of the fingers gives the Mudra the potency to heal. Let's look at the five fingers:

❑ The thumb represents the element earth, the stomach, and worry.

❑ The index finger represents the element metal, the lungs, and the large intestine and the emotions are depression, sadness and grief.

❑ The middle finger is the element fire, the heart, small intestine, circulatory and respiratory systems, and the emotions are impatience and hastiness.

❑ The ring finger is the element wood and is connected to the liver, gall bladder, and nervous system, and corresponds to anger.

❑ The little finger corresponds to water, the kidneys, and fear.

If you are overwhelmed by an emotion, just squeeze the corresponding finger a few times and you will feel better. It works!

In palmistry and astrology too the fingers depict profound meaning. The little finger is Mercury, the ring finger Apollo, the middle finger Saturn, the index finger Jupiter and the thumb is Mars. The soft padding under each finger is the respective mount. The soft padding under the thumb is the Mount of Mars and opposite it is the Lunar Mount. The Earth Mount is between the two, in the hollow of the palm, and the beginning of the palm, at the wrist, is the Mount of Neptune.

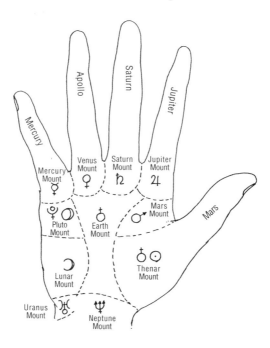

The little finger relates to communication, the ring finger to relationships, the middle finger to responsibility, the index finger to self-worth and the thumb to self-assertion.

The second *chakra* is associated with the little finger; the ring finger is associated with Apollo, the sun god, and the root *chakra*; the middle finger is associated with the throat *chakra*, the gateway of purity; the heart *chakra* is associated with the index finger; and the fire element and Mars are associated with the thumb. Every finger has energy and has a role to play in our well-being and development. It is often said that one's health is in one one's hands. Quite literally too, considering the awesome power given to each finger.

Very often, while healing with hands, one can feel tender, soft, even painful areas on one palm while roaming over them with the fingers of the other hand. These are pressure points and can mean that a certain co-related organ is disturbed or over-used. Gentle everyday touching normally helps. Overworked parts tend to calm, and underworked areas optimise. The fingers and the palms are, indeed, vital.

Esoteric Moving Mudra

This has to be done carefully and its effects are arguable. Place your thumb tip and middle finger tip lightly together and gently and slowly rub in a circle about ten times on the first section of the middle fingers of the other hand. Reverse circle ten times. When this is done correctly, you may feel a warm flow from your hands to the wrists, forearms, elbows, upper arms, shoulders and spine. When the spine is getting warm, move the thumb to the mid-section of the middle fingers. Repeat the procedure. The warm flow will move along the spine down to the end. Next, move the thumb to the base section of the middle fingers and rub accordingly. The warm flow moves from the pelvic to the upper legs, knees, lower legs, and ankles and to the bottom of the feet.

This is supposed to open all blockages and improve circulation throughout the body. Your body may feel hot. This Mudra is supposed to cleanse every illness out of the body.

Place your thumb on the side of the mid-section of your ring finger on both hands. Slowly rub up and down along the mid-section. Lighter the better. Now you may feel an expanding, warming sensation on the back of your head. This is supposed to help heal many illnesses like headache, brain tumour and brain atrophy.

The Chakras

We have mentioned the *chakras* prominently in the book. So it is important to know what they are all about and how they influence us. *Chakras* are vital in all sorts of yogic exercises and in some, like The Five Tibetans, all the yogic exercises are based on the core spinal energy of the seven *chakras*. If Christopher Kilham, the proponent, is to be believed, exercising the *chakras* or optimising *chakra* energy, keeps the body supple and youthful and staves off the marauding effects of old age.

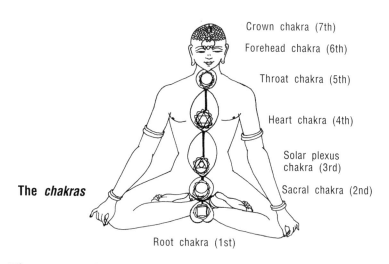

Crown chakra (7th)

Forehead chakra (6th)

Throat chakra (5th)

Heart chakra (4th)

Solar plexus chakra (3rd)

The *chakras*

Sacral chakra (2nd)

Root chakra (1st)

The seven *chakras* are the primary energetic centres. Located along the spinal pathway, each *chakra* is associated with particular organs, glands and nerve plexuses. Each *chakra* is also associated with certain states of consciousness. These seven *chakras* function in concert and can be balanced or imbalanced depending on the state of the body-mind. Peak *chakra* functioning is essential for a healthy, vital and balanced life.

The seven *chakras* lie along the spinal column and are connected by three major energetic pathways known as *ida*, *pingala* and *sushumna*. The channels run from the base of the spine to the top of the head, conveying energy from one *chakra* to another.

The first *chakra* is located at the base of the spine at the perineum, the spot between the anus and the genitals.

The first *chakra* is about survival, power and the promotion of vital life energy. Its Sanskrit name is *muladhara*.

The second *chakra* is located at the point of the spine close to the reproductive organs. Its primary functions are creativity and procreation. Its Sanskrit name is *svadhisthana*.

The third *chakra* is located at the solar plexus. It is all about personal power and is the vortex for the individualisation of consciousness. Its Sanskrit name is *manipura*.

The fourth *chakra* lies at the centre of the chest and is considered to be the focal point of love and compassion in the human energy system. Its Sanskrit name is *anahata*.

The fifth *chakra* is located at the spine directly behind the centre of the throat. It stands for creativity and personal expression. Its Sanskrit name is *visuddha*.

The sixth *chakra* sits directly behind the root of the nose, between the eyebrows and inward toward the centre of the head. Also called the third eye, this *chakra* is the location of higher intelligence. Its Sanskrit name is *ajna*.

The seventh *chakra* is located at the crown of the head and is the centre of cosmic consciousness. It is an unconditional state of total fulfilment, freedom and joy. Its Sanskrit name is *sahasrara*.

Chakra influences permeate the entire body and mind and work at every level. *Chakra* psychology is a tool for greater self-understanding. *Chakra* imbalances are endless and all of us are imbalanced one way or the other. Either we are not well rooted, too giving and selfless or we are too self-absorbed and ambitious, or we are somewhere in-between on some level or shade of imbalance.

The *chakras*, without doubt, play a vital role. I have been doing *chakra* meditation and exercises for over a decade, and the journey has been remarkable to say the least. The ecstasy that floods your being can only be experienced;

words are too commonplace to describe the energy that floats through your consciousness when the chakras are open and you are in a meditative trance.

With *chakra* energy, the calmness that spreads over the body-mind is exhilarating. In addition, the body is toned, ageing is arrested and the spiritual journey that I have been coaxed into has become a source of endless joy. *Chakra* energy is simply awesome and is the cornerstone of spiritual growth.

Osho, Tantra and Mudra

Osho, formerly Acharya or Bhagwan Rajneesh, blazed a controversial trail with his 'Sex to Superconsciousness' theory. A seer who attracted global attention with his easy, no-holds-barred approach to life, Osho advocated a life of abandon and passion. An iconoclast, he shattered accepted norms and gave sexual play, in particular, a new set of wings. Subjected to brickbats when he was alive, the world is looking at him with new eyes years after his passing away. Without doubt, Osho was an extraordinarily original thinker.

His ashram at Koregaon Park in Pune reverberated with an energy that shook even his greatest critics. The quality of his books, music and theatre was extraordinarily high, and the ambience at Koregaon Park was touched by an electricity that simply torched the visitor. Gardens, ponds, meditation halls and exercises of all kinds elevated the soul to newer reaches of knowing. Having spent quality time there, I was witness to the gigantic transformation that touched each and every one of us at different times depending on the scale of our personal evolution. Every seeker was rewarded, and we all came away in the knowledge that a master had touched our lives and we would never be the same ever again.

In the early eighties, Koregaon Park came alive to a whole new consciousness. Spread over large areas of well-cultivated land, thousands of devotees from all over the world flocked to India to sample the new 'curry' of a new age guru. Osho broke all rules and all accepted norms and bludgeoned his way to new theories of self-realisation.

He believed that to attain enlightenment, a person passes through four doors; he has to open four locks. Those four locks are called four seals or four Mudras.

The first Mudra is called the *Karma Mudra*. It is the outermost door, the very periphery of your being. *Karma* means action, which is the outermost core of your being; it is your periphery.

The first seal is opened by becoming total in your action. Do whatever you do with passion. Immerse yourself in it. Be one with it, let it consume you. The focus, the concentration, is also yoga. Lose yourself, be one with it. There will arise great joy in action. Osho reiterated the belief that if you are consumed by any sort of emotion or desire, allow it to flow unabated from within. Don't let it coil inside like a serpent waiting to explode. Allow it free rein. Let it vent, and get friendly with its fury.

If you are angry, be totally angry; you will learn much out of total anger. If you are totally angry and fully aware of your anger, anger will disappear one day. There will be no point in being angry anymore. You have understood it. It can be dropped now.

The same goes for love. Why is it said that young love is completely blind? It doesn't listen to reason and is stubborn and defiant. Try explaining away young love to the lovers lost in its vice-like grasp. Use reason and logic and tell them it won't work, and even a brick wall will appear compliant in comparison. Young love is almost always a folly; desperate love certainly always is. Try telling this to the lovers in question and no words could sound more foolish to young ears.

But don't intervene. Allow the lovers to journey the course of their love; don't stop it. They will be blinded by it. The fury of love will consume them, and they will emerge from it cured.

Once a person has been eaten by love, given his all to it, he will emerge from the flames a better human being; chastised and cured of it, ready to take on the challenge of life with an open heart. There is a new maturity. With it also comes a humility seasoned by the flames of love. This is *Karma Mudra*. Go fully with your emotions. Immerse yourself in whatever you do or in whatever you feel and be delivered!

Anything that is understood, that can be unravelled or fathomed, can be dropped easily. It's only when you don't understand it that it continues to grip you and pin you down. Like a mystery thriller. You simply can't drop the book until you reach a point where the mystery starts unfolding. Then there are no demons. Everything is unravelled and all the cards fall into place. When the issue continues to elude you, it becomes like a boa constrictor or quicksand. You struggle, it pins you down and draws you further into the mire. You struggle harder and the more you are caught in its vortex. So be total, whatever it is. Enter the passion with the force with which it aims to consume you. This is the first lock to be opened.

The second seal is called *Gyana Mudra* – a little deeper than the first, a little more inner than the first – like knowledge. Action is the outermost skin; knowledge is a little deeper. You can watch action but you cannot watch what is going on in another's mind. "Actions can be watched; knowings cannot be watched, they are inner." Actions are visible. But the mind is a monkey on a stick, and the worst part of it is that the monkey is not visible. The second seal is that of knowing or *Gyana Mudra*.

Osho says that one should start knowing only what one really knows, and stop believing things one is not sure about. Be honest with your inner self. Say only what you know and the second lock will be broken. If you go on knowing things and believing things that you don't really know, the second lock will never be broken. False knowledge is the enemy of true knowledge. The media and hearsay fill our minds with a multitude of beliefs and half-truths. False wisdom is passed on to finally attain dangerous and cult proportions, and no one knows where it all originated.

Osho exhorts man to drop all that he didn't know but believed that he did. "You have always believed, and you have always carried the load – drop that load. Out of a hundred things you will be unburdened of almost ninety-eight things – unburdened. Only a few things will remain there that you really know. You will feel great freedom. Your head will not be so heavy. And with that freedom and weightlessness you enter the second Mudra. The second lock is broken."

All belief should be convincing, not based on speculation or hearsay or lack of concrete evidence. Rumours, lies and false prophets come in packs and exploit the insecurities of badly formed minds. All the clutter that eventually seeps in can hurt, destroy and maim. So all the 'nonsense' should be discarded and space made for new beginnings.

The third Mudra is called *Samaya Mudra*. *Samaya* means *time*. The first, outermost layer is action, the second layer is knowing, and the third layer is time. Osho says, "Knowledge has disappeared, you are only in the now; only the purest of time has remained. Watch, meditate over it. In the now-moment, there is no knowledge. Knowledge is always about the past. In the now-moment there is no knowledge; it is completely free from knowledge. Just this moment, looking at me, what do you know? Nothing is known. If you start thinking that you know this and that, that will come from the past. That will not come from this moment, not from now. Knowledge is from the past, or a projection into the future. The now is pure of knowledge."

Samaya Mudra is to be in this moment. The past is irrelevant. Lessons are not normally learnt from it; instead dwelling on it can maim progress. Nothing is known of the future and barring making broad plans nothing else can be done with it. So what we are left with is the present and how well one handles it may well shape the future and eradicate the demons of the past as well.

In Tantra, according to Osho, only the present is time. The past is not, it has already gone. The future is not, it has not come yet. Only the present is. To be in the present is to be really in time. Otherwise you are either in memory or you are in dreams, which are both false and are delusions. So the third seal is broken by being in the now. Osho spoke of complete joy by being in the moment, which is not linked to previous regret or anticipated joy. Moments make life, and when moments are celebrated an entire life is celebrated. He believed in celebrating every moment be it death or divorce. The ashram connected to every nuance of every moment. Even Osho's epitaph read: *The man who was never born and never died.* So there was no room for sorrow; only continued, unadulterated, ever-cascading joy.

First, be total in your action – the first seal is broken. Second, be honest in your knowing – the second seal is broken. Now, be just here, now – the third seal is broken.

And the fourth seal is called *Mahamudra* or the great gesture. Now, purest space has remained. The previous three Mudras covered action, knowing and time. Space is the fourth Mudra. "Space is your innermost core, the hub of the wheel, or the centre of the cyclone. In your innermost emptiness is space, sky," says Osho. The fourth seal is space. These are the four seals to be broken. It is not easy. The journey is about self-awareness. "Great work is needed to go into your reality. Clarity is attained only when you have entered your pure space."

Tantras and Mudras

Tantras have almost always been misunderstood. Somehow Tantra and sex (not that there is anything wrong with sex) have always been clubbed together. Unfortunately, because of this, Tantra has attracted a lot of misdirected attention. Normally, the superficial or the most provocative, base and easily excitable, attract the average seeker. But Tantras, it is believed, have superseded the Vedas over a large part of India. Two-thirds of Hindu religious rites and at least one half of medicines are Tantric. There are different schools of Tantra. For the purist, the rituals of *Dakshinacarina* are considered to be in harmony with the Vedas, while the rituals of the *Vamacarins* are considered suitable for the more adventurous.

The teachings of the Tantras are based on the *Bhakti Marga*, which is regarded as superior to *Karmamarga* and *Jnanamarga* of the *Upanishads*. The doctrines of Tantra are derived from the *Sankhya* philosophy, mainly the theory of *Purusa* and *Prakriti* with a special emphasis on the mystic side of the Yoga. *Brahma* is *niskalpa* (non-differentiated) and *sakalpa* (differentiated). Tantra deals with *sakalpa* or *saguna Brahman* and its five main features are: *Bijamantra*, *Yantra*, *Shree Cakra*, *Kavaca* and *Mudra*. The *Panch Makar* whose names begin with the letter M (*Madya*, *Mansa*, *Matsya*, *Mudra* and *Maithuna*) – respectively meaning wine, meat, fish, parched grain and sexual union – have been interpreted literally as representing the five elements of *Hatha Yoga*.

According to Tantra, absolute reality has two aspects: *Shiva* (Male) representing pure consciousness and *Shakti* (Female) representing energy and activity. The truth regarding the union of *Shiva* and *Shakti* is to be realised within the human body while it is alive. This is a different approach from other schools of thought that claim that the truth is attainable only after the physical body has been shed.

In Tantra, the human body is a microcosmic universe. The spinal cord represents Mount Meru, while the three main metaphysical veins (*ida, pingala* and *sushumna*) running left, right and middle of the spine respectively, represent the three sacred rivers – Ganga, Yamuna and Saraswati. The breathing process represents the course of time.

The identification with sex is because *Shakti*, the female source, also called the *Kundalini*, lying serpent-like, coiled and quiet around the *Muladhara Chakra* (wheel) is aroused and made to move upwards to unite with *Shiva* (male). The sexual union represents the activities of the negative and the positive. The male resides at the *Sahasrara Chakra*, which is described as a thousand-petalled lotus at the top of the head. The union of *Shiva* and *Shakti* brings about the transcendental realisation of the absolute non-duality.

The Yogic Life as Accessory

Yoga is a necessary alibi in the elevation of consciousness. It is an ancient system of exercises and personal development for the body, mind and spirit and took birth in India over 5,000 years ago. With its gentle movements, deep breathing and long stretches it's an ideal method of relaxation and energising. There are also vigorous forms of yoga and you can choose the one most suitable.

Yogic exercises or *asanas* strengthen the nervous system and help the mind and body to optimise their potential. Through healing, strengthening, stretching and relaxing the skeletal, muscular, digestive, cardiovascular, glandular and nervous systems, the body is strengthened. Yoga helps the mind find a new calm and also prepares the body for meditation.

There are several schools of yoga. So many that you can even find one tailor-made for your specific needs. There are many difficult poses too, but it's not necessary to twist your body into any pose that isn't comfortable. Yoga is replete with deep breathing exercises called *pranayama,* and *nadi sodhanas* or alternate nostril breathing techniques, useful in relieving stress, depression and other mental and physical problems.

Yoga recognises the holistic nature of a human being and seeks to create flexibility and strength in all parts of the skeleton and muscles, while removing built-up toxins in the system. It seeks to maximise the capacity of the lungs to perform easily and without strain, increase circulation and oxygenation of the blood and massage the internal organs to maintain a constant outflow of toxins and inflow of life force. Yoga seeks to return the body to the flexibility and flow it was naturally born to.

Mudras are the yoga of the fingers. Holistic healing is all about harnessing the life force around us. A complete healing with Mudras is well within reach with a lifestyle change that can balance the psyche and soma and bring about a centre in our lives.

The Right Diet Helps

There are no real accessories necessary to practise Mudras. As we have repeatedly mentioned, they can be done anywhere and at any time and by anybody. But there is also no denying the fact that the right environment, the right thoughts, the right colours and the right foods go a long way in ushering consciousness into the healing process.

There are several diets and innumerable fads, which increase in number with every passing day. This is a global phenomenon and India is no exception. The media is replete with 'healing' diets and how it is best to go 'natural'. However, diets are personal and one needs to stray a bit before zeroing in on what is right. It is very individualised. Several new theories crop up all the time, and the human body is extremely complex and challenging, throwing up surprises like a genie.

Despite all this, there are certain ground rules that have stood the test of time. All the Mudra practitioners I spoke to have talked endlessly of a simple vegetarian diet used in moderation and preferably devoid of white sugar, salt, white flour and white bread. Tobacco and alcohol are consigned to the bin, water is drunk in large quantities and foods that ostensibly excite the body are avoided.

Foods do play a vital role in the nurturing of consciousness. Warrior races are not known to subsist solely on green vegetables quite like saints are not heavily dependent on flesh for

subsistence. The right diet, without doubt, feeds the right consciousness. So the regular and effective practise of Mudras will be greatly enabled by the intake of what can be referred to as 'healing' foods.

Macrobiotics is a healthy, holistic way of living a balanced lifestyle. In essence, it is a constantly changing holistic system that is ever striving for balance. It not only covers diet, but balance in body, soul and spirit.

The actual word *macrobiotic* originates from the Greek and means *great or large life*. It is based on The Yellow Emperor's *Classic of Internal Medicine*, the oldest-known book of Chinese medicine. It is attributed to *Huang Ti*, the legendary Yellow Emperor (born c. 2704 BC), but was probably not written down until about 500 BC. The Yellow Emperor is believed to have ruled China during a golden age and is considered the ancestor of all Chinese people. When borders opened and the world grew smaller with all the travelling, the diet spread to the western world and then reached every shore.

There are all types of diets on display today. Even vegetarianism has its distinct caste system. Plus there are different schools of alternate healing with their own diet prescriptions. For example, Ayurveda recommends a different diet for a *vata* personality that is far removed from what a *kapha* person should consume. But a macrobiotic diet seems to wear a universal, contemporary, thematic appeal.

As a part of nature, man needs to live in harmony and co-operation with it. This includes eating foods that are in season and from the area in which you live. A balance of *yin/yang* is what is sought after. Extreme *yang* foods, to give examples, are red meat, eggs and refined salt. An excess of these foods in a hot climate will most certainly wreak havoc on the body's balance. And then it will need to be centred with *yin* foods.

A strong *yang* condition caused by excessive meat eating makes us susceptible to anger, aggression, intolerance and impatience while a yin condition makes us weak-willed and impractical.

Another aspect of the macrobiotic diet is that our organs need different types of food on a regular basis to keep them healthy. The five main types are: sweet, sour, salty, pungent and bitter. Because the change in seasons also causes a change in the *yin/yang* balance of our surroundings, one's diet also needs to be changed according to the seasons. Nature also takes care of our requirements with its seasonal fruits and vegetables. All one has to do is observe the signs and follow a sensible diet plan which is natural and adaptive to the seasons. The way the food is prepared also changes its balance. Food can go very *yang* with more heat, pressure, time and salt.

Besides diet, macrobiotics includes a whole way of living. Physical exercise, the diagnosis and natural healing of unbalanced physical conditions, a good balance in ecology and the environment, art, recreation and spirituality are the essential condiments of the macrobiotics lifestyle. Gratitude, forgiveness, appreciation, faith and letting go are all part of it. It is a holistic approach to freedom from the physical and psychological chains of our lives. It is a deep acceptance of the goodness of all life, and the healing begins from inside.

Dr Vijaya Venkat, Kavita Mukhi, Jehangir Palkhivala, Dr Anjali Mukherjee, Rama Bans, Dr Swati Piramal, HK Bakhru, Dr Shah, the late Dr Jussawalla and scores of others spread all over the length and breadth of this vast and colourful country have coughed up hordes of diets. Milk, sugar, salt, white bread, meats and several other foods have got the stick. With marginal differences, there is an agreement on the broad principles of a healthy diet.

India is an ancient culture and holistic diets originated

here long before the rest of the world could possibly even smell it. Natural fasts and therapies and detox systems are as old as drought and famine. India is also possibly the mother of all Mudras. The reason I mention all this is because healing is a holistic process and if the practise of Mudras were accompanied by a soft, healing and consciousness elevating diet the healing process will be that much more complete.

of related interest

Body Intelligence
Creating a New Environment
2nd Edition
Ged Sumner
ISBN 978 1 84819 026 9

Eternal Spring
Taijiquan, Qi Gong, and the Cultivation of Health, Happiness and
Longevity
Michael W. Acton
ISBN 978 1 84819 003 0

Seeking the Spirit of The Book of Change
8 Days to Mastering a Shamanic Yijing (I Ching) Prediction
System
Master Zhongxian Wu
Foreword by Daniel Reid
ISBN 978 1 84819 020 7